C000133729

CREATING YOUR AUTHOR BRAND

A WMG WRITER'S GUIDE

KRISTINE KATHRYN RUSCH

WMG WRITER'S GUIDES

Creating Your Author Brand
Copyright © 2018 by Kristine Kathryn Rusch
First published in 2017 in a slightly different version on kristinekathrynrusch.com
Published by WMG Publishing
Layout and design © copyright 2018 WMG Publishing
Cover design by Allyson Longueira/WMG Publishing
Interior art © copyright andrewgenn/CanStockPhoto
Cover art © copyright andrewgenn/Depositphotos
ISBN-13: 978-1-56146-066-3
ISBN-10: 1-56146-066-4

CONTENTS

CREATING YOUR AUTHOR BRAND

INTRODUCTION

Every Thursday, I publish a blog on writing or the business of writing. I initially started the blog in 2009, and except for a six-month hiatus in 2014, I have written a post without fail every week. In the spring of 2017, I got the bright idea to write a short blog post on branding.

As I wrote the blog, I realized I had a larger topic than a single blog, but it wasn't until I started getting comments on that blog that I understood how large the topic actually was. Readers asked very good questions about things I mentioned in passing. I realized, as I read the comments, that what I thought was obvious, was not. Most people had thought branding was about book covers, and very little else. They had no idea how big branding actually is. Business and advertising majors lose entire semesters to branding classes. Branding experts get paid big bucks to "re-envision" an entire business, from the bottom up, just so that business can be marketed.

I wrote blog after blog, encouraging questions, because somehow, in my years in broadcasting and advertising, I had absorbed most of this stuff into my marketing DNA. I didn't know what other people didn't know. And in order to write about this to non-

marketers, I had to figure out what people—and writers in particular—needed to learn before they could understand some of the
major concepts.

If I wanted to make these posts useful, I needed feedback.

And I got it. You might want to go to the posts, which are still on
my website kriswrites.com, and read the comments. I answered a
lot of questions directly, and not all of those answers made it into
this volume. In subsequent blog posts, I answered the major topics,
but not the minor ones. (I have a life; I would have been writing
about branding and marketing for the rest of my known days.)

I have put this book together from those blog posts. I'm keeping
them in the order in which I posted them, and I'm keeping the
colloquial real-time language. Please remember, as I cite "current"
examples, they were current in 2017.

I wrote these blogs for writers. If you're looking for a great
overall book on branding, one that will help you brand your auto-
motive store or your online quilting business, this book will help
you understand the concepts of branding in simple language, but
there might be a more specific and on-point book for your niche.

Writers, publishers, both indie and traditional, will benefit from
this book much more. It is, I believe, the only book on branding
written with the publishing industry in mind.

A word on terminology: when I mention *traditional* publishing, I
mean the industry that grew up in the early 20th century in places
like New York and London, and publishes thousands of books per
year. Those businesses include international conglomerates and
large publishers that have existed since the 1980s at least

When I mention *indie* publishing, I mean the industry many call
"the shadow industry," which has arisen since Amazon's Kindle
entered the marketplace in 2007. *Indie* writers include writers who
self-publish, and those who publish through very small publishers
(sometimes started by the writers themselves, but which are a separate entity from the writer).

Most of what I write is geared toward indies. There are more and more indie writers every day, some of whom make hundreds of thousands of dollars per year without doing a lot of branding or marketing. Early on in the post-Kindle world, it was relatively easy for a self-published writer (who wrote good books) to make a small fortune at their writing with a minimum of marketing effort. Now, however, it has become harder to get discovered. (I wrote a book on that as well, called *Discoverability*.) One relatively easy way for readers to find a writer's work, however, is through branding.

Branding is the simplest way to gain reader recognition. Gaining that recognition is not as easy as putting an ebook up on the 2009 Kindle platform, but using branding to gain that recognition is easier than all those marketing tips from so-called gurus who appear for a year or so and then vanish when their way of gaming the system ceases to work.

This book will help you understand branding. The book will also help you figure out what to do for *your business*. If you're looking for a book that will give the Five Steps to Proper Branding —a kind of plug-and-play sort of book that gives you the Secrets to Quick Branding—this ain't it.

What this book will teach you are the basic concepts of branding. It will also open your mind to the possibilities of branding, of the various things you can do for your business. I hope the book will give you ideas, and make you want to dive deeper into the possibilities of marketing your work in a way that's as unique as the books you write.

In order to brand like that, however, you need to understand how branding works, how readers (and other consumers) respond to it, and what you can and cannot do to attract their attention.

This book is designed to give you that basic understanding and to help you convert that understanding into useful action that's right *for you*.

Ready? Here goes...

"I've just been spiffing up my image a bit."

IN THE BEGINNING...

I feel like I've been on a particularly grueling business trip, and am slowly recalibrating back into my office. I worked very hard in the front part of April as I prepared for the science fiction writing workshop I ran on the Oregon Coast.[1] Then the workshop happened. Lots of great discussions, great questions, great stories, and dedicated work later, we finished...and I got the Mother of All Colds.

I've been staggering my way through the past week, trying to rest and trying to do a few non-brainy things. The thing is, my brain, which is weird on a good day, is really weird when I'm sick. It takes all of the stuff that I've been thinking about, mixes it all together, and then comes up with connections that my healthy brain would never consider.

I value those connections, because they sometimes help me see things I missed—or missed writing about. In this case, I came up with a list for the Business Musings blog.

Before the workshop, I had been blogging about newsletters, so marketing was on my mind.

At the workshop, I talked to writers about the importance of

1

telling a good story as opposed to writing lovely sentences. And yet we focused on craft, too, the importance of the right sort of detail to make stories come alive.

And I'm still negotiating several TV/movie projects, which has been annoyingly distracting, considering 80 percent of them won't come to anything. At least two of the deals are for entire series, which got me and Dean to discuss the possibility of trademarking those series, and whether it's worth our time.

Then, in the middle of the workshop, two books arrived in the mail: *Fallout* by Sara Paretsky, and *The Burial Hour* by Jeffery Deaver. I was reading manuscripts at the time, and so put the books near my reading table as a reward for finishing the workshop. Paretsky has already made my Recommended Reading List on my website and, as I write this, I'm still enjoying the Deaver.

The thing is: I had forgotten I ordered the books. I certainly didn't know they would arrive during the workshop. That arrival was a very nice surprise.

And yes, this all factored into the soup of thoughts that whirled through my brain that last week.

I have read Paretsky since the 1980s and Deaver since the 1990s. I don't like all of the books Deaver and Paretsky write equally, but I like the authors enough to preorder, sometimes with only a title attached. It's never a gamble to order books from either of those writers. Both of them write fascinating stories that take me away from whatever I'm doing, even if the stories don't always work.

I have maybe a dozen books on preorder at any one time. When I finish a book by one of my favorite authors, I look on Amazon to see if the next book is available to preorder. If it is, I preorder it then so I don't have to think about it.

If I'm truly anticipating a book, I'll check that preorder occasionally to make sure I actually paid for the upcoming release because I really, really, really want that book. Generally, though, books just show up in my mailbox. Those books either wait for a moment or a mood—this winter, I couldn't read anything but Regency romance as friends, family, and cats kept dying around me —or, in some special cases, I read the book immediately upon receipt.

I am a customer—a loyal customer—of those writers whose books are on preorder. Or, in a few cases, I'm a loyal customer of a particular book series, but I don't care about other things that the author writes.

Amazon, bless them, sends me reminders when an author whose work I've ordered a lot writes a new book. I don't even sign up for the alerts. They arrive. I read them.

I do get a newsletter from a few of my favorites who have gone indie. That helps finding their books. But I've unsubscribed from more indie newsletters than I currently subscribe to. Getting an email a day (yes, one indie did that) was truly annoying.

I try not to send too many newsletters, although I sent a news-letter per month to two separate lists in the first six months of 2015 as my Retrieval Artist released. That was my big flurry, and it was tiring. It took some writing time.

I try to do newsletters when I'm brain-fogged, which means I wrote a couple this past week. I have promised on that list not to spam these folks, so I only email when I have actual news.

The first newsletter was for the fans of my Diving series to let them know that the newest book is included, in its entirety, in *Asimov's Science Fiction Magazine.* That newsletter copy is pretty short, but it is conversational. It gives the readers two pieces of information: *The Runabout* is available now in a magazine should you want to buy now. Or if you prefer to wait, then the book will be out in three standalone formats in October.[2]

The Diving list is pretty tight. It's been several days since I sent the newsletter. My open rate (for the emails that can be tracked by the silly algorithms) is steady, and no one has unsubscribed. A lot of folks clicked through the email links (which always surprises me, because I never click an email link. I just open a new window, go to whatever website, and find the page myself). The Diving newsletter had a good result.

Then I wrote my overall newsletter. [3] This newsletter is considerably longer than the Diving newsletter, even though it has some of the same information. I had a lot more to inform readers about than just the release of *The Runabout*. I also am in a writing Storybundle, along with nine other writers. I have even more to say than that, but I felt that if I dealt with much more, I'd be inundating people. Better to save some firepower for May's newsletter—whenever I get around to it. (If I get around to it. May looks busy on the writing side.)

Again, colloquial language, but more of it. And a weird design, because I have to keep myself amused somehow. Again, good clickthroughs. A few more unsubscribes than usual—but that was because I told people to unsubscribe.

What? you ask. Why would anyone tell people to unsubscribe?

Because I want the readers of a particular series, who don't want all the noise, to sign up for the newsletters for those series. That way I don't spam the readers. So I reminded everyone they could subscribe to a series/pen name newsletter, and then they could unsubscribe from this one.

According to the unsubscribe comments I got, about eight people took me up on that—and promptly subscribed to the other newsletters.

Yeah, yeah, I know. The newsletter gurus for writers say don't scatter your newsletter subscribers to more than one list. Because then your readers won't be focused on you and will have less chance to buy something else from you.

I figure my readers are both smart and know what they want. If they want to try something else I've written, they will. If they want a newsletter that tells them all of the publications, then they can subscribe to the big newsletter. And if they don't want to subscribe to a newsletter at all, they can see what I post on my website when I do a news post.

Which leads to the third thing I wrote in that cold-fogged week. I wrote a news post that appeared on Saturday. The post dealt with *The Runabout*, the bundle, and three short story publications I'd neglected to mention in the past two months. The post was even longer than the newsletters.

The responses have been great, and mostly in email or on social media. I've received questions about the Diving series from the fans, including some very thoughtful long letters filled with guesses about the future of the series. I've gotten some questions about other series (which always happens when I send out the big newsletter with only one series mentioned). I also got some great comments about the news post, including a question or two about the short story anthologies.

I love the interactions with the fans, but I also like the way they're engaging with the series. That means a lot to me personally, since my days are mostly spent sitting alone in a room and making things up. Those things matter to me, but it's nice to know that they matter to others as well.

I should have known that, because I am a reader and a consumer of stories, and I love series. Last week, I also spent way too much time worrying about the consequences for Our Heroes in the last storyline of the season for *Marvel's Agents of S.H.I.E.L.D.* So, yeah. Fans get invested. Readers do, too.

All of this thinking got folded into some other reading I was doing. Courtesy of Randy and J.T. Ellison, I received a copy of Targoz Strategic Marketing's Reading Pulse survey.[4] They wanted some comments on it before it went live, and I did a quick dive into the survey before the workshop.

As I read it, I realized I needed to spend a lot of time with this thing, because it's actual research on reading that's useful, not wish fulfillment. Here's how the press release describes it:[5]

Based on six years of survey research, the syndicated study provides book publishers, agents, and sellers with an accurate picture of readers, and delivers actionable data on what readers want and how to influence them to buy.

It does deliver "actionable data." I got very excited by what I read. I got permission to share bits of this with you, but I can't share all of it, because the survey isn't public. It's designed for larger companies with the resources to buy surveys like this. (That's how they get funded.) Randy says there will be a different version for indies that won't be as expensive. But that won't appear until after the big push for the survey to traditional publishers in the next few weeks or more.

This survey can be tailored to a particular company. If I were running one of the Big Five? Four? Three? Two? (who the hell knows) major publishers, I'd be plunking down the money for a customized version of this thing. Because there's a lot of information here that could change traditional publishing forever.

It won't, however. Even if traditional publishers buy this survey, they won't act on the suggestions inside. The corporate headwinds are too strong. A lot of what's in here would cost department heads their jobs, and devastate the sales departments. Of course, a lot of what's here would result in new hires as well, for new jobs that would have a completely different focus.

That kind of sea change is almost impossible in large companies. But in small ones, it's definitely possible.

I had avoided thinking about much of what's in the survey until after the workshop, when I thought I would have the brainpower to do a deep dive into the numbers. I have only had brainpower for a day or two. The deep dive is coming this week.

So what's been rolling around in my head isn't the proprietary numbers that I can't tell you or the changes I'm thinking about for my own business based on these facts. Instead, it's a section at the end of the survey that essentially has actionable information for Writer Me.

The section at the end talks about Brand Name authors. There's a long list of writers by genre that readers identify by name. And the survey found something that I was aware of, but not that I had really thought about.

Almost all of the Brand Name authors that readers are familiar with are traditionally published. And most of those Brand Name authors are baby boomers. Not just baby boomers, but on the upper end of the baby boomer scale. One genre didn't have a single person in the top ten brand names under the age of sixty.

I would normally dismiss that kind of finding as irrelevant. Writing is a career that many people start late. It's not at all unusual for "new" writers to be in their fifties, so by the time their name is established, they'd be in their sixties.

But I looked at the names more closely, and saw a completely different problem. The survey broke into four rather broad genre categories: Mystery, Thriller & Crime; Romance & Paranormal Romance; Literature & Literary Fiction; and Science Fiction & Fantasy. Then the survey noted the top ten most recognized names in each of those categories, chosen by readers.

Of the forty names on those lists, only three got their start in this century. Those three included two whose books were made into major movies, and one author who (as far as I can tell) jumped on the coattails of one of those two. (That's not something to be ashamed of in any way: John Grisham jumped on the coattails of Scott Turow, and eventually surpassed Turow in numbers of books published and recognizability and a whole bunch of other things.)

The remaining thirty-seven brand names were nurtured in a completely different publishing climate. One I'm not going to count because he's an actor, not an author, and I have no idea how he got on the list. So that brings us to thirty-six. Two got their start before 1960. Five got their start in the 1960s. Six got their start in the

1970s. The bulk got their start in the 1980s, with only two getting their starts in the 1990s.

(I'm doing this off the top of my head, so I might be wrong on the exact start dates for the previous century. But I do know for a fact that not a one of those thirty-six names got started in this century.)

That pre-2000 publishing climate allowed series writers to build. It also allowed writers who only wrote standalone titles (and there are several on these lists) to have lower book sales on one title but still buy the next.

In the 1990s, a publisher could let a series author go, and another publisher would pick up that author—and buy the series out from the old publisher, keeping all of the books in print.

From the late 1990s onward, traditional publishing stopped nurturing careers. It stopped trying to grow a brand name, and instead tried to create one. It's still doing that. As this survey noted, many of the authors on the Brand Name list now write books with co-authors, trying to boost the "younger" writer's career. (The survey did not count those books in this part of the total.)

Writing with a brand name does not grow a writer's career the way that nurturing a series does. It increases that writer's sales, but only for a book or two. If the publisher does not continue to help that writer by sticking with them through a number of books, that writer will disappear like everyone before them.

I studied those lists of names for much too long. I also studied the list of up-and-coming writers, noting that many of them are also over fifty. Many of those writers have had long careers, too, but they somehow managed to survive the purges and are now being recognized by readers.

Then I went to my Amazon order screen and looked at my preorders. I currently have sixteen books on preorder. Three are from the same author, a romance writer who is doing a series I love.

Two are from the same thriller writer. One is an anthology I've been looking forward to.

So...twelve authors on that unscientific list. Four got their start in this century. One started indie, but is doing a trad pub series now. All four of the authors who started in this century are romance authors.

All of them.

I read new writers all the time. I read a lot of anthologies and indie books. The preorder field only represents trad pub because I prefer to read in paper, and it's almost impossible to preorder indies in paper. So my preorder list is 100 percent trad pub—and very representative of the findings that the survey had.

I have been reading the eight authors since they got their starts way back when. And they've held me throughout some ups and downs. I'm a lot more forgiving than traditional publishing is, although I have been known to dump long-time authors after about five books. Two of the brand names on the survey list are writers I no longer read, so I miss them like you'd miss an old lover. I really want them to write books I love again. But those writers aren't writing what I love anymore. They both are repeating themselves, and I find their work dull now. Sadly.

So, the conclusion my cold-fogged brain served up to me was twofold. First, traditional fiction publishing in at least two genres is in a great deal of trouble. They haven't nurtured their new voices.

Second, because there's trouble ahead, there's going to be a lot of room for indie bestsellers to become brand names as these brand names die off or stop producing. Readers will be looking for something similar.

Not something manufactured. As I mentioned above, Grisham rose on Turow's coattails, but not because Grisham was trying to be Turow, but because Grisham—a lawyer—already wrote fiction, and Turow was a slow writer. Grisham filled the hole.

That's how brands used to start. At a bookstore, I would say, give me something like...Scott Turow, and I'd get hand-sold a John Grisham novel. This is happening in some bookstores with fantasy novels that are "like" Game of Thrones, because George R. R. Martin is so slow.

But there's more to it than being in the right place at the right time with the right book. It's *how* to be in the right place at the right time. And that has nothing to do with names on a newsletter list. It has to do with producing a lot of product.

The two-book writer on my preorder list? That's John Grisham. He's been producing two and three books a year for thirty years now. He's got a lot of backlist. And most of it (all of it?) is still in print.

That's something indies can do. We can keep our books in print.

But we need to brand them.

And that cold-fogged brain of mine realized that I have never dealt in depth with branding. Because branding is not just making a name big on the cover of a book or making sure all of the books in a series look the same. There's so much more to branding than that.

This is the introductory post, then, to a longer series on branding. It became clear to me after reading this survey that I needed a refresher. I also needed to give a lot of thought to branding, not just my names, but my series.

The Hollywood negotiations and trademark discussions brought that home, as well as the fan reaction to the newsletters. I gots me a lot of thinkin' to do, and I do that thinking best by writing.

So why not a series of blogs?

Which is exactly what I'm going to do.

"Sven, you are diluting the Viking brand."

TYPES OF BRANDS

I've been talking to myself lately. Actually, I've been talking back to podcasts, vlogs, and emails. Ever since I said I would be doing a series on branding, I've gotten links to great branding tips. (Please, keep them coming.)

Every single link I received that dealt with branding from a writer's perspective talked about cover branding. Lots of great information in each and every one of those blogs or podcasts or discussions, but every time the writers mentioned branding in reference to a cover, I would mutter, *There's more to branding than covers.*

A whole ton more. In fact, when I mentioned at the regular Sunday professional writers' lunch that I would be doing this series on branding, one of the wags across the room from me asked, *Without an entire semester? How can you do that?*

Very generally. Because as my fellow writers who also have MBAs know, branding isn't a one-off topic. Business schools have entire courses and majors in branding.

Branding, at its best, is an art and a science.

As I got ready to do this series, I went over to my favorite default, *Adweek*, only to discover that they only have five subtopics listed on the header of their website, and one of those is "brand marketing."

Okay. I promise. No entire semester. No gigantic course. But lots of information geared at making you think outside of the box that writing and publishing has put you in.

First, I'll start, as I always do, with a definition.[6]

According to Brick Marketing, which had the best pithy definition I could find:

A brand is the idea or image of a specific product or service that consumers connect with, by identifying the name, logo, slogan, or design of the company who owns the idea or image.

Sounds simple, right? But it's not. My usual go-to source for definitions, Investopia.com, has a long and complicated definition of "brand" that goes into some of the topics we'll discuss in future blogs (but not today). When Investopedia gets into the nitty gritty of the definition of a brand, it makes this very important assessment:[7]

A brand is seen as one of its company's most valuable assets.

I bet you never thought of your brand as an important asset in your business. I'll bet that, aside from "branding" your name on the cover of your indie-published book, you've never thought of branding at all.

The first thing all of these sites discuss in examining brands is "brand identity." As Investopia says, "A company's brand identity is how that business wants to be perceived by consumers."[8]

Investopedia hastens to point out that brand identity is different from brand image. Your brand identity is *how you want* customers to perceive your brand. Your brand image is *how customers actually* perceive your brand.

Yeah, yeah. Already too much detail.

Some writer blogs are savvy enough to know that the writer can be the brand. The publishers rarely are the brand. Harlequin was a brand once upon a time, although it has pretty much blown that by diluting its brand identity. Baen Books has a brand identity that's pretty consistent with its brand image—that of providing science fiction and fantasy to sf/f fans in the know.

Over the years, publishers have had brand identity that coincided with brand image, but as more and more mergers occurred, publisher brands got swallowed up or disappeared entirely. What does Penguin Random House stand for now? Who knows? Not even they know.

Branding is marketing on an advanced level. Some of it does concern names on the cover. Some of it concerns the way a writer gets perceived. Some of it concerns a whole bunch of other things.

Back in the days when traditional publishing reigned supreme (and dinosaurs roamed the Earth), writers left branding up to their publishers. The people who interacted with the writer—editors—didn't know anything about branding. The sales force generally took charge of the marketing, and wouldn't even consider branding an author until the author had already had some success.

At that point, the sales force would tell the editor that the writer should probably stick to a particular type of book (say, books about tiny robots), because that was the writer's perceived brand. But aside from that kind of malarkey, and decisions made in the art department about the size of the name on the cover, traditional publishers rarely, if ever, thought about branding.

Which is just plain stupid, considering that writers partner with their publishers so that their publishers will handle the marketing.

But I digress.

So as indie publishing grew, and the writers who had the most experience with marketing turned out to be the hybrid writers, they talked about what they knew: names on the cover, making sure the stories remained the kind of stories readers wanted from that writer, and so on and so forth.

Leaving, as my poker player husband would say, tons and tons of opportunities on the table.

Realize, before I go any farther, that this series of blogs isn't for you. It's for me and for the people who work with me on my books. Because I know all this stuff and I've been too damn busy to apply it to my own work outside of a throw-spaghetti-against-the-wall-and-see-if-it-sticks kinda way. Some of that is because I spent the last eight years clawing back the rights on my traditionally published books. Some of that is because I've been simultaneously building five different businesses at the same time.

And some of it was because I didn't feel ready yet to do this kind of marketing push.

But now's the time.

I have to admit, though, that it took Randy Ellison and his Targoz Strategic Marketing's Reading Pulse survey[9] to kick me over the top. There's a lot of good information in that survey, things that I need to implement in my business. I was planning to do this, with some extra research under my belt, in the next year or so, but the survey kicked me forward. I will discuss some of its conclusions when I get to that point in this series. However, if you want to see some of the conclusions, go to The Hot Sheet, sign up for their 30-day free trial, and click on the May 3, 2017 links[10]. (By the way, they have some great material as well, almost every week.)

Randy's work made me realize how haphazard our work has been on my publications, as well as on Dean's, and the publishing company I co-own, WMG Publishing. We moved toward branding and marketing a few years ago, but dropped that as we reorganized the business. We're ready to do so again, with people who are invested in learning about this aspect of publishing.

But marketing isn't as simple as some of the writing blogs make it sound. As I said in *Discoverability*, you need to know what your target audience is. You also need to know exactly what it is you're marketing. And that's where branding starts.

According to one business website, there are eighteen different kinds (types) of brands. I went over there and yeah, they're right, there are a ton of different kinds of brands. But most aren't relevant to what we're discussing here.

Some business courses cite ten different kinds, but the consensus seems to be that there are somewhere around five, six, or seven different types of brands.

For our purposes here, we'll go with six different types of brands. They are:

- **Service**
- **Personality**
- **Product**
- **Organization**
- **Event**
- **Geography**

Let's start with the two I'm going to dismiss as irrelevant to writers. (Most of the time. All of this is most of the time.) Geography refers to places that need to brand themselves. "What Happens in Vegas, Stays in Vegas" is one way that Las Vegas branded itself. New York has billed itself in a variety of ways, from the city that never sleeps to "I [heart] New York." Virginia, on the other hand, declares that "Virginia is For Lovers," and New Mexico is "The Land of Enchantment."

That's branding on a **geographical** scale. Sometimes that's relevant to writers because some writers (like Linda Fairstein) become inextricably tied to a particular setting or place, but it's rarer than you'd think.

Event refers to big repeating events, like Burning Man or South by Southwest. These things become brands, and they're centered around some kind of experience that people will have jointly. The Chicago Blues Festival is an event brand.

Some writers do event branding—particularly if they're doing something special with a book tour. A few years ago, Gallery Books put ten of its romance authors on a bus and made the bus tour into an event. The bus had a special logo, just like the tour did. Called "Belles on Wheels," the bus tour became an event, and the promotions began months before, including drawings, big reveals of tour dates, and of the bus itself.[11]

Had Gallery Books done this Belles on Wheels tour every year, it would have become an event worth branding, the kind that readers would have looked forward to. It might have become something that the press noticed, something that communities planned for, and something that actually benefitted the authors who were on tour.

It did not. It was a one-time event, not an ongoing event, so it became less of a big deal than it could have been.

Other writers did some of this branded event touring on their own dime. For the life of me, I can't track down the marketing on these things with my handy-dandy Google. (A brand, by the way.)

Mostly, though, the brands that will matter to us as we go through this series are:

- **Organization**
- **Service**
- **Product**
- **Personality**

Most of the marketing advice concerning branding that you hear for writers is about **personality** branding. (Some places, like the Dummies site[12] [also a brand] differentiate Person brands from Personality branding. Yeah, yeah. I'm not going to get as technical as I can, okay? If you want that, follow the links yourself, and dive into that rabbit hole headfirst, like I did.)

Personality branding is pretty straightforward. The person brand is focused on a famous person, while the branding is all about the personality. This works for groups as well as individuals (think Kardashians). The biggest personality brands belong to people like Oprah or Martha Stewart or Emeril Lagasse.

Sometimes a person becomes so famous they become a brand whether they want to or not. (Cher, Prince, or any one of a dozen celebrities at any time in history.) But generally speaking, the personality brand was nurtured by the personality herself.

The biggest personality brand that I know of in romance is Debbie Macomber. Everything she does, from her books to her speaking tours, reflect who Debbie is—or at least, how she presents herself to the world. For a while, James Patterson had a personality brand. He's in the process of diluting it by writing with co-authors and doing a bunch of other things that we'll discuss later.

Stephen King, on the other hand, has a personality brand that he doesn't pay much attention to. If he did, he would only write horror fiction. Yet, his name is recognizable and his brand is the diverse fiction (within certain limits) that he writes under that name.

Organization brands are just that: branding done for organizations. The Red Cross is a brand. A lot of organization brands are tied to personality—a charity started by a famous person, for example, might become an organizational brand in and of itself.

Publishers are organization brands. Your indie publishing house could become a brand. Baen Books is a brand that sells itself as a brand. So does Tor Books. So did Harlequin, but since Harlequin was bought out, it doesn't do so any longer. Eventually that organizational brand will simply go away.

Service brands are based on the experience, on what the consumer gets—the service, if you will. If you're run a house-cleaning business, you're providing a service. If you do it well, then you will eventually get recommendations based on the name of your company.

A service brand is based on trust. The consumer has to believe that the service they will get from the brand will be good—or at least good enough.

Uber is a service brand: in theory, you can trust that app will bring you a car that will get you from one place to another safely. Considering many of the problems that Uber has had, it still hasn't entirely mastered the trust part of a service brand.

Writers aren't just a personality brand. They're also a service brand. Writers who become Big Names provide a guaranteed service—the reader will get an enjoyable escape from their reality for a few hours. Even if the book isn't up to the Big Name's highest standard, the book will still be good enough that the reader won't regret the purchase.

Product. Certain products have brand awareness. 7 Up is a brand and also a product. If you buy 7 Up in Dallas, and then buy another can of 7 Up three months later in Detroit, you expect the exact same taste experience.

A product brand can be an individual item like a can of soda or it can be a series of items, like Ford trucks, all built to the same standard, and all with the same expectation of quality. I'm not saying the product is good; that depends on your taste. But the quality of the product(s) should be the same across the board. One brand-new Ford truck shouldn't be impossible to drive off the lot while the other model of brand-new Ford truck drives like a dream.

Writers can have product brands, which I will get to shortly. If a writer writes a successful series, that series becomes a product brand.

Businesses can have different layers of brands. The business can be (and often is) its own brand. The business might also have a personality brand. For example, Virgin Atlantic has Richard Branson, who is a personality in his own right.

For those of us in Oregon, we deal with the personality of Phil Knight, the co-founder of Nike. In Oregon, Phil Knight and the Knight family are both a regional brand (yes, another kind of brand)

and a personality brand. Outside of the state (and outside of American sports), most people have not heard of Phil Knight, although they have heard of Nike.

Nike is an organization brand, a business brand, and if you shop in their stores, a service brand. Their products, though, have their own branding, which gets very esoteric.

Sometimes the products share branding. When Michael Jordan was the face of basketball in the 1980s, he got an endorsement deal with Nike to produce a branded shoe—the Air Jordan. Those shoes were so popular that they are still being produced today, even though Jordan himself has not played professional basketball since 2003.

Highly successful writers often end up with three different kinds of brands, whether they know it or not. Those writers are personality brands. They also are service brands (for providing a specific kind of read). And, if they're known for a series, they end up with product brands as well.

Sometimes this happens accidentally. George R. R. Martin was very well known in science fiction when he sold his fantasy series to HBO, but he became a three-way brand once the show hit the airwaves. George did a lot of media (and he's funny), so he became a personality brand. The series books ended up being product brand, even though George has written a bunch of other books outside of the series. And for better or worse, he has become a service brand, although at the moment, that part of the brand is mostly known for not finishing books on time, which isn't really helping the brand much at all.

Most writers who either still exist in traditional publishing or started there end up with their brands accidentally. They lost control of the brand creation early on, so what they end up with is their brand image, without ever giving thought to brand identity.

Some writers focus on branding from the beginning.

Lee Child is very clear about the fact that he chose his pen name with an eye toward branding. In an article titled "Lee Child" written by Oline H. Cogdill in the Holiday 2016 issue of *Mystery Scene*,[13] Child called his name change a "show business thing." But he thought about that "C" last name and chose it for a marketing reason.

"When I started," he said, "there were a huge number of authors whose last names began with a C. I wanted readers to see my books as quickly as possible."

In the interview, he intertwines service with product, and discusses both of those brands (without using the word) in a single paragraph. He said, "I sort of have an emotional contract with the reader. They want Reacher, and I think it would be upsetting and weird if I put out a book without Reacher. And even if it was the greatest book, I don't think readers would accept it."

Other writers write more than one series. A number of brand name writers, Stephen King and Dean Koontz among them, write books in more than one genre. But they don't really think about intertwining branding and bringing the consumer into the art.

Child does.

It's all a choice about the kind of writer you want to be, and the kind of work you want to do.

I believe that a writer should write what she wants (even if it is the same series with the same character) and then worry about marketing that material. Because of the haphazard nature of my own career for the past twenty years, I have too much varied material, and I need to separate it out so that readers can find what they want and what they're looking for.

"Kristine Kathryn Rusch" can be a personality brand for some consumers, but I'm better off marketing my Rusch books as both service and product brands. Readers will get a promise from me for the Diving series, that it will never be set in 2017 here on Earth. They get a different promise from me for the Retrieval Artist. And so on and so forth for all the series I write under Rusch.

I have an easier time with Kris Nelscott, one of my pen names. I'm not ever taking Nelscott out of gritty historical mystery that deals with issues of race and gender. There, my work will resemble Child's—I know that Nelscott readers want a particular kind of story and that's what they'll get.

The same with Kristine Grayson. That brand is goofy paranormal romance. If Grayson were to write a gritty 1960s detective novel, she would be breaking faith with her readers.

Rusch doesn't have those constraints, but that creates its own problems, as I mentioned above. Although I do give branding some thought with the name.

One reason I changed the name of this blog from the Business Rusch to Business Musings is that I didn't want my last name constantly associated with the word "business." Of course, I didn't think of that when I founded the business blog in 2009, so the name change was a course correction.

The Business Rusch is much more memorable than Business Musings, but I don't want memorable on the title of this blog. I just want it to be a side thing that I do.

The first thing we writers have to do as we figure out branding is what kind of brands we provide. Are we personality brands? Service brands? Product brands? All or none of the above?

Because that will matter on how we market things, and how we use our brands to good effect.

So during the week, figure out what kind of brands you already have. If you don't write a book series, but you have a large readership, you probably have service and personality brands. If you write a series, add in product brand. If you have more than one series, you probably have more than one product brand. And if you have pen names, then you might have more personality brands.

You need to know who you are and what you have before you can leverage any of that.

The other homework I'm giving you this week is to pay attention to the brands around you. Not just the brands from writers, but from companies. As I wrote this blog this afternoon, I was hyper brand aware. I noted the brand on my TV, the brand in my tablet, the brand of tea that I drink, the brand advertised on my T-shirt, and the brand of the laundry detergent I was using.

Brands are everywhere now, and we pick the brands we use for a variety of reasons. Keep track of your reasons, because your consumer choices will influence how you market your own products. Make a list of what you like and don't like.

Because you need some brand awareness as we go deeper into this series, and doing those simple things will help you with that awareness.

Until then...

"And you say we paid the agency how much for this slogan?"

HOW TO BUILD A BRAND: THE EARLY STAGES

When I do marketing posts, they tend to freak my loyal readers out. Sometimes, the posts freak me out, too. What writers want from marketing blogs are simple suggestions that boil down to this:

Do x, y, and z, and you'll get these fantastic results!

Only it doesn't work that way. Or rather, it doesn't work that way for everyone. I'm writing this on Sunday, after our weekly professional writers lunch. We have writers of different levels at the lunch, including writers who've worked for decades, and writers who are on their third or fourth year as full-time professionals.

We discussed Amazon ads, which we all jumped into at roughly the same time, using the same or similar methods. We all have had stunningly different results. Those of us who've been in the business longer haven't seen the uptick that the newer authors are seeing—which makes sense, since the ads are about information and discoverability, and we're better known.

Besides, the hot new thing in indie publishing marketing is only the hot new thing for a few weeks or a few months. Then everyone jumps on the bandwagon and the hot new thing becomes tepid. The innovators move on to other things, hoping some of those things will become hot, and everyone else waits for the xyz instruction on what to do next.

Sorry, folks, you won't find the hot new thing here. This book doesn't provide a list of prescribed steps requiring exact action to guarantee success.

I don't guarantee nothing.

I am going to add one very important caveat, which will be in each and every chapter: if you bring any of this marketing stuff into your writing—your storytelling, your creative process—you are screwing up big time. You'll ruin the very thing your readers love about you.

Your readers love your ability to surprise them. Your readers love the fact that you take them on a journey that seems both familiar and unusual. If you do what you believe your readers want, you'll retain the familiar and jettison the unusual. You will never be able to surprise them again.

You will ruin your art.

Marketing is not about your writing art. Marketing is a separate art, one that will take study and diligence—and, most of all, patience.

I know, I know. You all want something that will bring results immediately. So do I. But building a brand is not about going fast or cutting corners. It is about continuity, reliability, and establishing your place in the market.

So please, please, as you read this book, do not bring the marketing ideas into the place where you actually write and create the stories that are uniquely yours. Once you've finished those stories, then you can figure out how to market and brand them.

In the previous chapter, I discussed the types of brands. If you haven't read that yet, I suggest you do so.

Writers who have been in the industry a long time or who have more than one series or use more than one name might have many, many brands.

I will deal with that down the road. The information in this post will apply to *all* of your brands. I'll be giving you a lot to think about, though, and if you have a lot of branded items, you might get overwhelmed. That's a warning.

After I posted the previous chapter as a blog, a few of you asked (in the comments and in private) when is the right time for a writer to start branding her work. Well, here's the thing. The moment you publish your first piece, you've begun branding. Branding happens whether you do anything or not. (Traditional publishing has relied on that aspect of branding for decades now, letting brands develop by themselves and then jumping on them once they're already established.)

Brand image—the way that customers perceive your brand—begins the moment a customer (reader) reads something of yours. That customer will get an impression of what you do, and that impression can be reinforced with other work.

If you're the kind of writer who writes one character or one series, then your branding will focus on that singular thing. However, if you're the kind of writer that I am, the kind who writes in multiple genres and in many styles, then you will have a brand image that focuses on variety and, perhaps, surprise. The readers, however, will define the specifics of your brand for you.

Think of it this way: you might describe someone's work by saying, "He writes all over the map, but his stories always have happy endings" or "Her stories are always filled with great characters, no matter what genre she writes in."

You can help brand image along by creating a brand identity. If, for example, you write fantasy and mystery, your fantasy books might have one look and marketing scheme, while your mysteries have another.

Those of you who are just starting out will have both an easier time of this and a harder time. Easier because you have less material to work with, and can shape the handful of things you've already done into a marketing campaign. Those of us with a lot of material and a history in traditional publishing will have a great deal of work that was mismarketed or allowed to die a horrible death or doesn't reflect what we're working on now.

For the sake of this chapter, though, let's pretend we all only have one brand. Just one.

We now need to build that brand—not with what we write, but how we bring what we write to market.

To build the brand, we have to do some things that are simple to say and very hard to do. I'll give you the list, and then I'll explain.

1. **Define Your Business**
2. **Define Your Target Audience**
3. **Research Similar Businesses**
4. **Figure Out What Makes Your Brand Unique**
5. **Figure Out What Your Brand Is Not**
6. **Create A Brand Mission Statement/Tagline**
7. **Be Consistent**
8. **Be Patient**

There are a million other things involved in building a brand, and we will revisit this part of the topic as the time comes. That's why this chapter is subtitled "The Early Stages."

So, let's go through the list from a writerly perspective.

1. Define Your Business.

The definition here is not "I am a writer." You must be more specific than that. Start globally and work your way to the specific. And you must think about this from the outside in, not the inside out.

Rather than "I am a writer," you could say, "I write the multi-volume Made-up World Fantasy Novel series." Or "I write award-winning short science fiction." Or "I write sexy contemporary romance novels set in Venice."

You might have an actual agenda, like some writers I know. Some write to give their readers an escape. Others try to improve the world around them. Still others present diverse characters in a modern setting, or characters who are differently abled and heroic or from some group underrepresented in fiction.

Some writers don't have an agenda, and simply write.

One way to figure out how to define your writing business is to ask people what they associate with your work. Is it a marvelous voice? Great characters? A unique milieu?

Your business definition is something you will continually refine over the years, so you're not completely stuck with it. If you want to understand how business definitions evolve, read *Shoe Dog* by Phil Knight, the founder of Nike. In many ways, that book is about the evolution of a brand. Nike went from selling other people's shoes to creating shoes to selling apparel and other sports-related items, all the while maintaining the uniqueness of the Swoosh (the brand symbol).

Your business definition will evolve over time, just like your business will evolve over time.

2. Define Your Target Audience.

When you're starting out, you won't have an audience. You'll only have a target audience. Those are the people you want to sell to. If you define your target audience as "all readers," you won't sell to any readers.

When I got the rights back to my Kris Nelscott novels featuring African-American detective Smokey Dalton, I knew immediately that my target audience was African-American readers. I know that's strange to say, given that the series was traditionally published, and those readers should have been high on the priority list for my traditional publishing company.

But that company had no idea how to market books with an African-American protagonist and, I believe, had no idea that there were African-American book clubs, magazines, and bookstores. (Seriously.) So the moment I reprinted those books myself, I made sure that they were advertised in various African-American outlets. That has led to a steady growth for the series and the Nelscott name (which, I admit, are two separate brands, but the instruction applies).

Your target audience might be people who loved the *Guardians of the Galaxy* movies. Or people who love World of Warcraft. Or people who collect Disney comics.

In the spring of 2017, KFC published a romance novel in which Colonel Sanders is the romantic hero. (I am not joking.) I'm assuming the target audience is romance readers who eat KFC. I also have a hunch that this was a great marketing ploy someone came up with, because I saw news about this novel in everything from *Adweek* to *The Washington Post* to romance blogs. And here I am, giving the book free advertising as well.

The marketing ploy worked. Will it work for Taco Bell? Maybe. But if Taco Bell does it, and MacDonald's does it, and Arby's does it, eventually readers will stop paying attention and will move onto the next big thing.

So define your target audience. And go as narrow as you possibly can. You want to be specific here, not general. The more specific you can be, the easier it will be to build your brand.

3. Research Similar Businesses.

By similar businesses, I do not mean similar writers. You work in the entertainment industry, folks. So look at what others in the entertainment industry are doing. What you're writing might be closer to the Sandman graphic novels than anything anyone else is doing in prose fiction. Or maybe you're writing books that are like *Sherlock*, the BBC's modern take on Sherlock Holmes.

It will be better for you and the brand you're building if you can pull ideas from outside of the publishing industry, or even from outside of the entertainment industry. Perhaps, like romance writer Sarina Bowen, you're writing books about hockey. Maybe your marketing should bring in elements of NHL marketing and elements of romance marketing. How do you brand that? Research and find out.

4. Figure Out What Makes Your Brand Unique.

Chances are you started writing to fill a niche that no one else was filling. You loved 1970s Gothic romances, and they went out of print. Now you're writing Gothic romances for the new century, with strong heroines and brooding heroes. Or Gothic romances for the LGBTQ community. (Oh, that sounds good.)

When I talked to George R. R. Martin as he was developing the fantasy novel series that became Game of Thrones, he talked about writing historically accurate epic fantasy. If the world was built on a medieval society, then it needed to have medieval values and medieval cleanliness, and medieval violence. (I think he achieved that.) Those ideas were revolutionary in the genre back in 1993-1994. The made-up fantasy worlds back then had more in common with wish-fulfillment than they did with the historical past.

Again, drill down. Figure out what makes your work unique. If you aren't writing in a series, figure out what it is about your writing that makes it yours.

Writers trained in traditional publishing have a tough time with this, because they're trained to say what their work is similar to, not what makes it unique. Forget the similar to part. Focus on what's different.

The more specific you get, the harder it will be for you to see what makes your work yours. So enlist the aid of others who love what you're doing. They'll tell you what makes your work special. Then you need to believe them, and run with that.

5. Figure Out What Your Brand Is Not.
You have probably said it, and have probably said it forcefully. "My novels are about a Cold War spy, but he's not George Smiley." "I write novels about crime scene investigation, but I write about the real crime scene investigators, not that magic stuff they did on CSI." "I write novels set in space, with an Empire and people fighting the Empire, but I try to keep the series based in science, unlike Star Wars, which is more fantasy."

And so on and so forth.

In this category, I often think about the comic *Get Fuzzy*, which is about a single guy living at home with his nasty cat and his very nice dog. Sounds just like Garfield, right? Only Garfield is gentle, and Bucky, the cat in *Get Fuzzy*, is a tiny little psychopath who rains terror on everyone near him. (I'm sure there are many other differences, but I haven't read Garfield in years. I prefer the Buckster.)

6. Create A Brand Mission Statement/Tagline.
The brand mission statement really helps, particularly if you can do it in a paragraph or a single line. It depends on what part of your business you're trying to brand. Debbie Macomber, for example, has been called "the official storyteller of Christmas," but that's only for one series of books. (They've been made into Christmas movies for the Hallmark Channel.)

My own pen name, Kristine Grayson, has a tagline which I did not think up myself (dammit). That tagline was one of the few good things to come out of my final Grayson traditional publisher. The tagline is "It's not easy to get a fairy-tale ending."

Yeah, that needs tweaking. (I hear Dean bitching about the passive voice as I type this.) But the idea is right, since the books are fractured fairy-tale romances.

Come up with something like that, something that can be as identified with your brand as "Just Do It" is with Nike's, and you'll really have a winner.

7. Be Consistent.

Most writers completely misunderstand this one. They think it means write the same book over and over again.

Instead, it means write the best book you can. Be consistent in your commitment to quality, whatever quality means to you.

If your books need to have a happy ending to satisfy you, then make sure they all have a happy ending. If you're writing historically accurate Westerns, make sure that you don't commit horse opera under that name. Or if you do, make sure you're clear: Cowboy Dan, known for his historical accuracy, throws caution to the wind and writes a dime novel filled with exaggeration. He hopes you have as much fun reading it as he had writing it.

With that, Cowboy Dan is acknowledging that the consistency in his brand might not be the historical accuracy, but the Western time period.

Once your business is defined, once your audience is defined, and once you know what is unique about your work, then you know how to make sure your audience senses the consistency— even as you change things up.

Consistency also applies to marketing. Make sure that if you decide on a logo or a typeface for your book covers that you use that same logo everywhere, and keep the typeface consistent. Your series books should be visually related to each other. And if you do visual ads for those books, those ads should resemble the books in some way even if the ads don't use the same art.

If your books are upbeat, make sure your marketing is upbeat. If you're writing humor, make sure the marketing is funny. If your books are dark and brooding, make sure the marketing is dark and brooding.

If you're consistent throughout your marketing, you'll reinforce the brand itself.

8. Be Patient.

You can't build a brand overnight. You can't even modify an existing brand overnight.

You can start branding, and you can make headway, but brands take years to develop.

I love how Raoul Davis expresses this in his article, "7 Keys to Building a Successful Brand" on the BusinessCollective website.[14] He writes:

> Be patient with your brand. Take on every new outreach initiative with care. Think of it as your baby. Just as you wouldn't start feeding solid food to a 3-month-old, don't rush any of your outreach activities, whether they be PR, advertising, or marketing materials.

He's right. Some of the things I'll do for my long-established series would be completely wrong for your brand-new series. But it's even more complex than that.

Brands and businesses morph. So do writing series and writing careers. I know many a writer who started in one genre, burned out, and moved to another. Some writers found their voices later. Janet Evanovich started as a romance writer, but felt constrained by the genre. She wrote twelve romance novels before she invented

Stephanie Plum, the character who made Evanovich's bestselling career.

In the previous chapter, I asked you to think about your brands. I also asked you to up your brand awareness, by examining the brands you use and the ones you ask for by name.

Your homework this time is to pick one of your writing brands (if you have more than one), and see if you can analyze it using the tools above.

Don't be surprised or upset if you can't find answers easily. That's normal. This is a whole new way to think.

Be patient with yourself. And think about this: the experts in marketing always talk about "building" or "growing" a brand. You don't build or grow anything overnight.

One step at a time, one idea at a time.

And whenever you're feeling overwhelmed, set the marketing aside, and do what you love. Go back to your writing office, forget this marketing stuff, and escape into one of your stories.

Because without those, this branding stuff means nothing at all.

"We've decided to market this product to disgruntled 25 to 54 y.o. women in bathrobes."

DEFINE YOUR TARGET AUDIENCE: THE EARLY STAGES

I love my blog. I love it because the readers make it so much better with your questions and comments.

When I posted the previous chapter as a blog, I got an unexpected result. In that post is something that seems pretty straightforward to me—the phrase "define your target audience." Some of you remarked in the email and the comments that you've been struggling with this one thing for a very long time.

Oh. What a revelation to me. When I write these blogs it becomes clear to me sometimes just how many things I do automatically.

I've worked in retail since I was sixteen years old. I owned my first retail store at the age of twenty-one. I currently am co-owner of three brick-and-mortar retail stores and um...three?...five?... online retail stores (it depends on how you count some of my businesses).

For me, finding a target audience is like putting on socks in the morning. The socks are in a drawer, I open the drawer, give the choice exactly three seconds of thought, grab the right pair, and go.

The rest of you don't see a single sock drawer. You see one of those sock collages where every sock that the photographer can fit in the scene is presented along the floor, in a beautiful and colorful pattern. Yeah, that takes tons of work. And no, that's not what I mean.

Thank you, thank you, thank you for bringing this step to my attention. It is hard to define your target audience if you've never done it before. And I had forgotten that entirely.

Let's start as basic as we can.

What Is a Target Audience?

A target audience is a specific set of people to whom you want to market your book.

I know, I know. You want everyone to read your book. But if you step back and think about it, you know that you will not achieve that, no matter what you do. Not everyone reads, for one thing, and not everyone reads all genres or all the writers in a particular genre, for another.

You need to drill down into who you want to market your books to. Once you figure out who you want to market to, then you can figure out how to market to them.

Why Does Choosing a Target Audience Matter?

Choosing a target audience matters so that you can tailor your marketing campaign to that audience.

This weekend, I had dinner with a group of friends. We were talking about TV and movies, and one friend asked me if I had seen *Get Out* yet. She thought I would love it.

I said I don't find humor in the situation they were presenting.

She looked at me like I was nuts. Humor? she said. It's a horror movie.

I said all the marketing I saw called it a comedy. Then she really looked at me like I was crazy.

We discussed the movie (heh! Word of mouth) and I decided, yes indeedy do, I would love to see that film. Absolutely. Based on what she said, not on what I had heard from the marketing.

When I got home, I decided to double-check. Had I actually seen marketing that said this film was a comedy? Turns out, I had never seen the trailer, which looked like a generic bad horror movie trailer (which wouldn't have appealed to me either).

So I looked at the online and print press, and saw headlines like this: Jordan Peele on making a hit comedy-horror movie out of America's racial tensions, and an entertaining and clever satire that is equal parts funny and terrifying. On and on and on.

No one I spoke to that night mentioned that the film was funny. Not a single soul.

On that level, it was a marketing fail, probably done because Jordan Peele is best known as a comedian (or was, until this film did well). The trailer, though, which I just watched, does appeal to horror audiences.[15]

That's a proper target audience for the film.

You can have more than one target audience for your product, but I'll get to that in detail in a future post.

If you know who your target audience is, you can talk to them directly, in a language and a tone that would appeal to them.

You see examples of marketing directed to target audiences all the time. During the United States football season (fall) in 2014, the National Football League finally figured out that it had a demographic it had never targeted before—women. Ad after ad featured women watching the games (not serving food like they did in the past), buying gear, and dressed in clothing with a particular team's logo. Some of this was because of the scandals that had engulfed pro-football (and the NFL wanted women on its side), but a lot of it had to do with studies that had shown that 46 percent of all NFL fans were women. And until those studies, the NFL had ignored that particular (large) portion of its audience.[16]

The NFL made a significant change, with some pink merchandise that supported breast cancer awareness, and a variety of female apparel from maternity jerseys with team logos to form-fitting T-shirts to leggings to just about anything else you could imagine. Fantasy football advertising showed women beside men choosing teams (or women in groups cheering on their teams). The change has worked and continues to work, growing the audience, despite the controversies still engulfing the sport.

That's just one example of targeted marketing. There are a million others. You target audiences all the time without thinking about it. It's as natural as breathing for you.

How? Well, my friends targeted an audience in that discussion. They believed that I would love *Get Out*. I needed to see it, and they hard-sold it to me.

In that same conversation, discussing some TV shows, the speaker apologized to another person in the room, knowing that person wouldn't be as interested in the topic as everyone else was.

We know our friends. We know which friend to share the gory novel with, which friend can only tolerate sweet romances, and which friend reads nothing but nonfiction. You wouldn't foist a sweet and unbelievable romance on the nonfiction reader any more than you would give the sweet romance reader the gory novel.

Find Your Target Audience Without Research

Later, we'll discuss how to refine your target audience or even expand it through research.

But right now, most of you have no idea who your target audience is and you're flailing about trying to find your target audience.

You're looking outside your writing room, seeing no one lined up to read your work, and wondering how to find your audience when you have no audience at all.

You're doing it backwards.

You've finished your novel. Now, take that novel from your creative office into your marketing office. (I'm using a novel here because it's a finite thing. We'll discuss career branding and marketing later.)

Figure out what that novel is. Fantasy? Science fiction? Urban fantasy? Steampunk? Drill down, figure out your subgenres.

Then, figure out what the book focuses on. Are the characters Chinese-American? Native American? Is the book set in Chicago? Does the book have all female characters?

Any one of those factors might focus your marketing. Two of them focuses it even more. Three of them helps tremendously.

So...your novel is steampunk set in Chicago featuring Chinese-American characters. Your target audience might be readers of Amy Tan or Ken Liu. You might look for book clubs that focus on books with Chinese-American characters or themes.

Or you could focus on the history of Chicago, and market to the Chicago media in one way or another. Would Chicagoans like seeing a steampunk version of their city? I think they might. Or would they like to see how the Chinese were treated when they settled in Chicago over a hundred years ago? Perhaps.

Try it. You can drill down your marketing that specifically.

Pick just one target audience to start. And then...

Tailor your marketing message to that audience.

How do you do that? You put yourself in that audience's shoes. What will appeal to them? When the NFL targeted its female fans, it didn't show them hosting hen parties while the men scarfed snacks in the living room. That would have talked down to women. Instead, it created products specifically for women and then marketed those items to women. Some of the ads for the Super

Bowl featured women, cheering as vociferously as the men usually did.

In a really good (albeit a bit too advanced for our purposes) article on defining a target audience, the authors Neil Patel and Aaron Agius interviewed Yaro Starak of Entreprenuers-Journey.-com.[17] They asked him how to build an online presence. He immediately focused on targeted marketing, and started with this:[18]

> I'd first focus on establishing a crystal-clear empathy with the audience I was planning to serve, so I know what their problem is, how they feel about it and what they currently do to try and solve it.

Empathy. You're writers. Find out what the readers you've targeted like and then put yourself in their shoes. Figure out what would appeal to them as well as what would turn them away from your product.

Talking down to those women the NFL wanted to target would have destroyed the effort the NFL made. Someone, somewhere, spent some time figuring out what parts of the NFL appealed to women, and then pointed the marketing in that direction.

Yes, sometimes that takes research, and we'll deal with that in a future chapter. But just as often, all it takes is a bit of thought and a whole lot of empathy.

Traditional Publishing Marketing

The thing that started me on this branding series was the Targoz Strategic Marketing reader survey, because in it, the data Randy Ellison compiled showed over and over again that most of the stuff traditional publishing does as marketing doesn't work at all. It's clueless marketing, based on ancient assumptions.

If you're following the traditional publishing path, you're probably doing marketing wrong. If you're doing what every other indie writer is doing, you're probably doing marketing wrong.

You have a unique product and you have (or will have) a unique brand. You have to make that work for you.

It sounds so easy, and it's not. It's a hard thing to do.

Which means…

You will get the marketing wrong.

More often than not, you might target an audience only to find they really don't give a damn. Or while you're targeting one audience, a different audience for your work has developed.

I was surprised when I went to book signings ten years ago that a major audience for my Smokey Dalton books was expatriate Southern white women raised in the 1960s who, as children, were not allowed to walk into African-American neighborhoods.

Time and time again, I talked to these women, who loved the books.

Later I figured out what had happened. St. Martins Press, terrified that a white woman had written a novel about an African-American detective, had tossed the first novel into the sink-or-swim mystery marketing channel. Had I been African-American, they would have marketed the book to African-American audiences only.

Instead, St. Martins hid the book from African-American audiences. Which meant that the readers who picked up the book were often white. And the white women who found it probably would not have gone to the African-American section of the bookstore, so to those women, this book was unusual.

The African-Americans who found the books loved them, too. But that audience grew slowly, which surprised me at the time.

While I worried that African-Americans weren't reading the book, a whole different audience was growing that I hadn't seen until I went to some signings and gave a few talks at mystery gatherings.

This is what happened with the NFL. They marketed 100 percent to men, and only gradually realized that half their audience was female. Whoops.

What do you do when you discover an unexpected audience?

You can do several things. You can retool your entire marketing strategy for a different target audience. Or you can do what the NFL did, and add in a completely different marketing campaign tailored to the audience you just discovered that you had.

It's Okay To Miss

Your target audiences will shift over time. Some of that will happen naturally given what you're writing. Some of it will happen because of world circumstances. For example, in an article about the development and marketing of *Get Out*, there's this little tidbit:[19]

> Conceived in the Obama era, Get Out *hits theaters with even greater resonance now...*
>
> *"This movie was intended to call out racism in what many people were calling a post-racial era," Peele said. "People didn't want to talk about race. Now, it's an undeniable part of the discussion again."*

Target audiences change. Or grow. If steampunk suddenly becomes as hot as apocalyptic fiction did a few years ago, then you would tailor your Chinese-American Chicago steampunk marketing to include the new target audience who had just discovered steampunk.

Specific, specific, specific.

The more specific you are in defining your audience, the better chance you have at building readership. Readership grows outward from one reader to two, two to three, three to four, and so on. At some point, the readers will end up doing the work for you, like my friends did for Jordan Peele. My friends targeted me as the audience; your readers will do the same for you.

So, as you search for your target audience, don't focus on the audience you do or don't have at the moment. (We'll deal with that aspect of this down the road.)

Focus on the audience you want. The audience you believe is perfect for the book you wrote. The audience who would appreciate it more than anyone else will.

Talk to those people in language that respects them—and language that interests them.

Yes, this will require some thought on your part.

And since I've been assigning homework, let me assign something here.

Instead of fast-forwarding through ads on your favorite TV shows, watch those ads. See if you can guess what target audience those ads are going for. You can test your responses by looking at the demographics for that particular show after you've done your guesswork. You'll see how well that show is doing in an age group and income category.

But I'll wager you'll see that in the ads without even looking at the demographic information.

And let me give you a mighty big clue: listen to the background music. Usually it's a hit song from a particular time period. If you know the time period (say the 1990s), you know that the ad is appealing to customers who are in their late thirties and early forties. The theory is that familiar music will make the viewer more receptive to the product.

(In my case, the hit song from my era often pisses me off at the product and makes me yell *I'm not that old!* at the TV, which is the indoor equivalent of *Get off my lawn!*)

I hope I answered those of you who asked about finding your target audience. Subsequent chapters will have more on this. But, please, do this work first.

BRAND IDENTITY

After the previous chapter went live as a blog, a lot of people had questions. Most of them appeared in the comments of that post. I answered most of those comments on that post, which you can still find on the website.

However, I chose to answer one in the body of the next post, which is this chapter on brand identity.

One thing I will say is that most of you seem to think of your audience as a thing, not as a person. As I said in the previous chapter, you start with one reader, then get another, and another, and another, to build an audience. In that sense, musicians have it better than writers.

A musician plays to empty bars. A musician watches as patrons come in, talking and laughing, and pay attention to their friends. Eventually, someone looks up and watches the musician. Then that someone elbows his buddy or shushes a friend to hear the end of a song. The friend starts listening. Then someone else notices that the two of them are listening. And soon the entire table is listening.

That's how an audience builds. Some of those people might return to hear that musician the following week. And the musician, remembering that moment, might play the same song or something similar before going on with her set list.

Your audience is not a thing. It's people. (Every time I type that sentence, I think of *Soylent Green*. That's not what I mean, though.)

As you find your audience, imagine people or a person or a table in a crowded restaurant, all of whom are slowly starting to pay attention to you. Make your audience real *to you*.

My inclination as a completist is to write all of the target audience posts at once, but that won't help you, because you can't understand some of the upper-level marketing stuff without understanding other basic branding concepts.

Also, I can tell from the questions I'm getting, both on the site and in my email, that many of you have not read *Discoverability* or the previous chapters. There's an attitude that you need to have in your marketing that most of you are missing.

Most of you want instructions. Do X and you'll get this result. Do Y and you'll get that result. I'm sorry, folks. Once we're past marketing basics—and branding is upper level, not basic—then that kind of talk is just silly.

Almost everyone who is selling a marketing system for writers is selling what worked for them at a very basic level. (Probably getting them from zero sales to a hundred sales or something small like that.) Once those people start talking about their success and boiling it down into a system, they become marketers only, and not writers. Those folks are selling a system that is as worthless to you (outside of a few stealable tricks) as any system promoted on late-night infomercials, with just as much hype and disappointment as those systems usually provide. Those systems are a get-rich-quick scheme—for their creator. Not for you. You're the one handing over the money.

I've said before, and I'll say it again: you will not get a system here in this book. You will get a way to approach branding and a way to think about it. The mindset is the important thing, because trends change. But marketing is something that has been around since the birth of capitalism. Marketing is flexible. You have to be, too.

Once you learn the mindset, then you have to do the hard work of applying it to your writing.

If you have trouble even conceiving of that, I'm afraid I can't help you beyond this: ask yourself why you have put up mental barriers on this particular topic. Why don't you want to learn how to do it right? Why don't you want to learn the mindset that will enable you to be flexible as trends change? What, exactly, are you resisting?

In order to do the upcoming posts on targeting your audience, I need to continue getting into the nitty-gritty of thinking about brands. You need some basics before you can move to how to use some of this to target audiences effectively.

Remember, the overall topic of the series is how to build a brand. In order to do that, you'll need to understand some basic concepts.

I must confess I didn't know some of the actual terminology before I started writing this as a series of blogs. I did know the concepts, but that was because we had to use them in my varied jobs. I didn't go to business school nor did I work for an ad agency or any large corporation that was organized around terminology. (When I formally worked on advertising, I was in radio, and we were shorthanded, so everyone did everything.)

So, in this chapter, we hit one of those terms that is completely obvious, but I hadn't ever used before in conversation.

Brand Identity

Brand identity is how you want customers to perceive your brand. You define the identity, although the customers may not accept that definition. (The customer's perception of the brand will appear in a different chapter.)

Right now, remember, we're dealing with building the brand. (If you haven't read the chapter "How To Build A Brand," go read it now.)

So you get to think about how you want that brand to be perceived. You need to imagine your target audience as you develop your brand identity. What do you want your target audience to think about your brand?

Remember, you're *building* a brand. You probably don't even have an audience yet. But you have a target audience—people you hope will buy your product. Those are the people (yes, people) you imagine as you decide how you want them to perceive your brand.

Let's start wide with the overall steps to building a brand identity, and then I'll refine for writers below. (Please don't skip ahead.)

Overall Steps to Building Brand Identity

Sounds so simple. Elementary steps that are (ahem) very similar to figuring out your brand.

But…let's have Investopedia really freak you out. Here's what they say about building a brand identity:[20]

> *Building a brand identity is a multi-disciplinary, strategic effort; every element needs to support the overall message and business goals. It can include a company's name, logo, design; its style and the tone of its copy; the look and composition of its products; and, of course, its social media presence.*

That freaks me out just reading it. Do I really have to do all of that?

Yep.

Over time, though. Not right away.

And remember, you don't have to get it right the first time. You can modify, change, reconsider, and redevelop your brand at any point in your business's history. Remember how I told you in some previous posts that I've been dealing this year with a lot of Hollywood types who are interested in my science fiction? Turns out one reason why is that Syfy is "refreshing" its brand.

Apparently, some genius at Syfy believed (years ago) that reality TV was the way to go. Now, Syfy is jumping on the scripted series bandwagon because of the streaming afterlife. Syfy mostly missed that boat and now needs scripted content immediately. Hence people are contacting me to see if my sf book series are available for option. (Everyone wants science fiction right now, not just Syfy, but Syfy's rebranding efforts are relevant to us here.)

Here's what Syfy is saying:

The network's reboot, which rolls out on June 19 (and globally later in the year) will include a new logo and typeface, but is much more than just surface level. "This is a wholesale change, top to bottom," says Alexandra Shapiro, evp, marketing and digital, entertainment networks, for NBCUniversal Cable Entertainment.

Go to the article from the link in the endnotes,[21] and enable video so you can see what they're doing with their logos—and yes, I mean logos plural.

Syfy is also returning to its roots. The "re"brand is actually a return to the original brand, in many many ways. (I remember when the channel started, because a friend of mine was influential in putting the channel together, using the vision Syfy is coming back to now.)

So...don't worry as you start into branding. Everyone rebrands eventually, especially when the branding isn't working the way you want it to.

The key is to start setting up your brand identity, and work forward from there.

If you go to that *Adweek* article on the Syfy channel, you'll also see how the channel is taking its overall brand and breaking it down for each subset—the TV audience, the internet audience, the social media audience. You'll also see how Syfy is using the new branding on the TV shows themselves.

Remember, each TV show has its own brand, brand identity, and marketing strategy. Marvel's *Agents of S.H.I.E.L.D.* took its branding one step farther in the 2017-2018 season, and divided the season into three story arcs, each with its own brand.

You can do all of that with your writing. It just depends on how creative you are.

So let me boil brand identity down for writers, as much as I can without getting too specific. (Remember, you can do this your own way. You don't have to use mine.)

I'm going to go from the small to the large, because it's simpler to write about—and probably because that's how writers will create their own brands.

Brand Identity For Writers

A Book:

Most writers just brand their books. Writers don't think about their entire business. So let's start with branding a single book.

Note: I'll be doing all of the following on the fly, as you should when you start spit-balling your branding ideas.

I'm going to use my standalone first novel, *The White Mists of Power*, as the example. We haven't really done much overall marketing with this book in recent years. It was heavily marketed by one of the last master marketers at a major publishing house when the novel first appeared in the early 1990s.

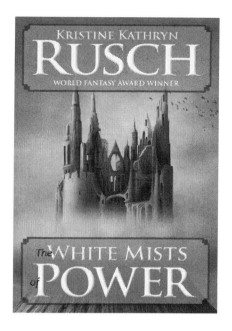

Definition

The White Mists of Power is what used to be called a high fantasy novel. The labels are more fluid now. For our purposes, the book is set in a made-up world with kings and queens and peasants and magic, but no magical creatures. It shares certain elements with George R. R. Martin's Game of Thrones series, but it lacks elements as well. *The White Mists of Power* is not a series book. It's not as dark as George's books (although my book is not light), and my novel doesn't have dragons.

The White Mists of Power is adventure fantasy fiction with appealing characters in a made-up world, with a lot of magic and a lot of politics.

Target Audience

Off the top of my head, the target audience is: people who liked George's books/TV series; people who like Ursula K. Le Guin's Earthsea; people who like Jacqueline Carey and Victoria Aveyard.

And as I type those names, I realize that in addition to the usual fantasy readers as my target audience, *The White Mists of Power* could be marketed as New Adult. That's an audience that wasn't even defined twenty-five years ago, and it would be new to this novel.

Personality/Voice

The novel's voice is pretty straightforward. The novel's not humorous or light in any way, although it does have music running as a subtheme. The voice is pretty close to my normal voice, so if I were marketing the book, I would use my usual speaking voice.

Brand Message/Tagline

Tougher to do here, off the top of my head. But I'd do something involving politics and growing up. The original tagline, appropriate to 1991, was "An Epic Fantasy About A Bard's Quest For His Stolen Inheritance."

Basic Branding

All of the marketing here will follow the look of the book itself.

Possible Out-of-the-Box Marketing

In addition to the usual stuff—cover branding, blurbs, using key words that would reflect the books I cited above—I might do a

Spotify playlist involving music similar to what I would think that Byron the Bard would play. The Spotify playlist would have a thumbnail icon that would either be similar to, or be a small image of, the cover of the book. I would do a few other things that might bring in readers 18-30, who wouldn't even know that the novel exists.

A Series:

Let's go with something very different here. When I first planned this post, I was going to use one of my sf series, but I think my Kris Nelscott Smokey Dalton series is a better teaching tool.

Definition

The Smokey Dalton novels are crime novels, set in the late 1960s/early 1970s with an African-American detective. They are straight private eye fiction, but set in a world rarely seen in modern mystery fiction (even now). The books are historically accurate and veer into noir.

When the books first appeared, the only similar series was by Walter Mosley. His Easy Rawlins series spans decades, though, and is set in a different part of the country. (L.A. for him, and Memphis/Chicago for me.)

Both series are very political, and use historical events as pivots for the mysteries. The Smokey Dalton series is critically acclaimed and award-winning, and has received attention, not just from the mystery press, but the mainstream press as well.

Target Audience

Mosley's readers, of course. Readers of George Pelecanos, because he also uses historically accurate backdrops and African-American characters. James Sallis's readers.

More than those readers, though. African-American readers, not just those who read mystery, but those who read historical fiction and historical novels. Readers of political fiction (and nonfiction) set in the 1960s.

Teachers, librarians, and an audience I've wanted to build—museum bookshop curators. I could easily see these books in the gift shop at the National Civil Rights Museum in Memphis, for example. I suggested this to my traditional publisher, who laughed. WMG will eventually try for this, but hasn't yet.

Personality/Voice

Very serious. Very political. Very focused on equality. Very focused on history as it relates to 2017. If Kris Nelscott/Smokey Dalton was all I was doing, I would be tweeting (more than I do) and writing blogs about Black Lives Matter and Voting Rights and Chicago Southside politics.

Brand Message/Tagline

Again, tough to do off the top of my head, and unlike *The White Mists of Power*, this was something my traditional publisher failed at. I think the tagline would probably be something about Smokey himself—a man who takes justice into his own hands. It would take some refining to get to exactly what I want here.

Basic Marketing

All the Smokey Dalton books have a similar cover design, with different (but similar) art, the same font, the same interior, and a similar pattern to their back covers/interiors. If you look at the books separately, they should appeal to a reader all by themselves. And if you look at the books together, you would see that they are part of a series.

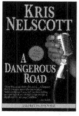 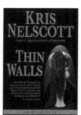 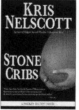 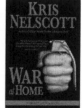

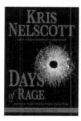  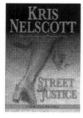 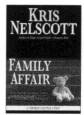 

Possible Out-of-the-Box Marketing

I already mentioned the museum shops as possible outside-of-the-box marketing. There are a lot of book festivals that target African-American readers, and I would see if I could get the books on their recommended lists. I would also do articles/advertising/blogs in publications/websites that focus on Civil Rights, the past, and the future.

The Writer Herself:

Initially I was going to use me (Kristine Kathryn Rusch) here, but I'm going to use Kristine Grayson because she's a much more typical writer than Kristine Kathryn Rusch is. Grayson moves outside her genre a little, but not all that far. (Unlike Rusch who goes from nonfiction to noir to goofy fantasy romance to hard sf to damn near anything else that strikes her fancy.)

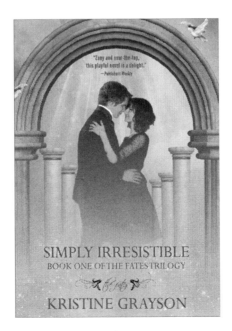

Definition

Kristine Grayson writes goofy paranormal romance and occasionally goofy fantasy short stories. She writes some YA novels, which are straight fantasy only, about the characters in her romances, and one Middle-Grade short that should have a few more added in. She also has a tongue-in-cheek Western series featuring a married couple that only exists in short fiction right now, but will probably be a novel series at some point. I'm also hoping to write goofy fantasy mystery novels with a romantic element using some of the characters from the Charming series of books.

Grayson has overlapping novel series—the Charming series, the Fates series, and the Santa series. They're unified by the weird use of magic and the irreverent tone. They're also all romances.

Grayson is non-traditional paranormal romance, without shifters and raw sex. Her romances are sweet romances (with some sex, mostly fade-to-black), her mysteries are soft-boiled rather than hard, the YAs don't tackle social issues (hard, anyway), and the books are all tied together by an off-kilter fantasy world in which fairy tales are real.

Target Audience

Readers who want to relax, smile, and not think about the problems of the world. Even with the upcoming mysteries, and in the YA novels, a happy-ever-after ending is guaranteed. Readers can come to Grayson to escape a bad day or a bad year.

Back when I was traditionally published as Grayson, I asked my trad publisher to target the audience of *Once Upon A Time* and other fractured fairy-tale kind of TV shows (there were a lot at that point).

The publisher didn't, of course, going only down the romance trade channels, which kinda sorta worked...badly.

Personality/Voice

Goofy, strange, weird. The voice is very strong (and often contradicts itself—or goes off on tangents [Grayson loves tangents] and silly side angles), filled with puns and lots of uncomfortable punctuation (rather like this sentence).

If I were only writing as Grayson, my social media presence would be a lot like the paragraph above. I would also be sharing fun, goofy things—nothing political, nothing dark, and nothing that does anything more than help the readers escape a bad day.

Brand Message/Tagline

Brand message: Everyone needs a happy ending.
Tagline (needs refining): It's not easy to get a fairy-tale ending.

Basic Marketing

All of the Grayson books should have a similar look, but each series should be branded to each other. Maybe the Grayson books would share a font with the author name. Or maybe the similarities would be in layout. (Name always at the bottom, or something.) The books should be recognizably Grayson, though, even if the series are different from each other.

Possible Out-of-the-Box Marketing

Marketing to fantasy readers, especially those who like fairy tales. Maybe even a somewhat different edition that appeals to readers of a different genre.

Genre/Subgenre

If you write a lot of standalone books in a particular genre or subgenre, you can do the kind of marketing I mentioned above for those books, making them a brand by genre/subgenre, even though they stand alone. Think of the Syfy channel here, and how it will be marketing its sf shows.

Or the CW channel, which has a superhero brand going—deliberately—and they cross market (with crossover episodes and everything) deliberately.

That's thinking outside the box.

A Business:

If you have a separate publishing business that publishes your writing, you will need to have different branding and logos for that business. That business will need all of the other stuff—the mission statement, the look, the taglines, and yes, even its own voice.

Thinking about Brand Identity for Writers

I used the examples above just to show you how you should be thinking about your own brand identity. Sometimes you can do all of the above—different brands, different attitudes. Sometimes you can roll the brand identity into one entity, often the writer herself. But that can trap you into one product or one genre.

That's what happened to the Syfy channel. They went too deep into one kind of product, and ultimately it hurt them and lost their core audience. They're rebuilding to recapture that audience.

If you think of yourself as a TV channel, like Syfy or the CW, then you can figure out how to craft your brand identity. Some TV channels have a lot of different programming with different tones (think ABC or the BBC). Some focus on only one thing, like some of the family channels.

Each programming item has its own brand identity as well, but that identity has to mesh with the channel's identity on some level. And then there are the standalone shows—the movies, the specials. Figure out how they fit into the channel as well.

There must be a vision behind your brand identity. Isolating and articulating that vision is 90 percent of branding. Then you can move forward with all of your other ideas.

Since I've been giving you homework, here's some:

Figure out what possible brands you could have. You don't have to do the write-ups that I did above. Just select what kind of brands you're interested in from your own work, and give some general thought about how you would begin your brand identity work.

Good luck!

"Now give us your spontaneous response."

BRAND IMAGE

The publishing industry has been shifting since 2009. Indie publishing has become a force since 2011 or so. At first, we writers were excited simply to make all of our work available. Then we started to do a bit more. However, things that worked six years ago don't work now.

The problem is that the marketing gurus for writers are just other writers with an okay idea. As I've said all along, we writers must accept that we're small business owners and start acting like it.

One way we need to act like business owners is to accept the responsibility for the presentation of our products. I've been writing about that for a few years now, but I've also known that I haven't done everything I could.

It took a few other things to push me forward on branding—not just cover branding (which I dealt with in *Discoverability*) but also with branding the way other businesses do it.

I've been idly noodling on all of this branding stuff off and on for weeks. Some of it comes from planning this series, but most of it comes from where my careers stand at the moment.

Branding is a new area for writers, particularly on the level that we've been discussing throughout this series.

It's something we all need to learn how to control and understand. We're in this same boat together. We're now in the position where we can apply general business practices to our writing.

When it came to branding, writers couldn't do any of this work before.

Here's why:

Until the indie revolution, writers ceded all of their promotional efforts to traditional publishing. Fifty years ago, the branding that traditional publishing did was for their own publishing companies. I'm currently reading Robert Gottlieb's book *Avid Reader*. The first section on his career at Knopf is particularly fascinating—and particularly applicable to this series.

Gottlieb worked at Knopf after Knopf's brand had become synonymous with quality literature. The attitude the readers, critics, and booksellers took toward Knopf was that whatever they published was excellent. (I remember this: I grew up in a snobby literary household. A lot of the books we bought were Knopf books —and they were good.) Previously Gottlieb had worked at Simon & Schuster, which had a different reputation.

He writes about the perceptions of the two different companies (and the impact on the work he did) this way.[22]

... I had come to realize that I was not the only one for whom the Knopf name had always held great resonance. Once the house began to show renewed energy, there was no difficulty attracting writers to the home of the Borzoi. The quality of our design and production was a further attraction. Perversely, at first I found this phenomenon unsettling—even a little irritating. Nina [Bourne] and Tony [Schulte] and I had spent so much energy trying to convince the publishing world that Simon and Schuster was a place of distinction—"Please pay attention to A Legacy! *Please try* Catch-

22!"—that we weren't sure how to behave in a situation where everything we published was presumed to carry distinction because we were...Knopf. It was particularly unsettling when books of ours that definitely lacked distinction nevertheless received the benefit of what was something of a free pass. We got used to it, however, the way one always gets used to being spoiled.

What he is writing about here, very clearly, is brand image. Brand image is the way that the customers *perceive* the brand, not the way that the business *markets* the brand. (I'll have a more extensive definition below.)

Back when Gottlieb was at the height of his editorial powers—the early 1960s through the mid-1980s—the publishing companies had distinctive voices and personalities. I remember reading an essay from Stephen King back in the 1980s, when he discussed how much he wanted to be published by a particular company because it was a prestige company (not something that published schlocky genre fiction). I remember feeling both happy that he confirmed my opinion about the company, and concern that he would change his own personal writing style to get into that particular company. (I worried needlessly. He did get the literary acceptance—in this century—for the work he was doing, not the work he thought he should do.)

Traditional publishing companies no longer have the kind of brand recognition that they enjoyed fifty years ago. All of that is due to mergers. The imprints have vanished, the brands are gone. In looking up that Stephen King quote—which I did not find—I saw that he is published these days by Scribner, which was F. Scott Fitzgerald's publisher ninety years ago, and still run by the Scribner family. (The company was founded in 1846.)

In 1978, Scribner merged with Athenaeum. Athenaeum merged with Macmillan in 1984. In 1994, Macmillan merged with Simon & Schuster—yes, the very company that Gottlieb once worked for, and which was once trying to convince the world that it published quality work.

Scribner still tries to hold onto its literary reputation, but it doesn't have one—not in the way it did in the mid-20th century. Its identity has been horribly diluted by all of this merging and messing with the brand.

The same with Knopf. It went through two different mergers in the past twenty years, and while the publisher is still identified by its Borzoi colophon, it doesn't really have the cachet it once had.

Why is this important to what we're talking about here?

Because the attitudes formed in the period of time when publishers had distinct identities still inform writers today. Writers still believe that a publisher will help them promote a book—and one way the publisher used to help promote was with the publisher's own brand.

You knew what kind of book you would get from Harlequin, from Knopf, from Scribner, from Pocket Books. With a handful of exceptions, that is no longer the case.

Buried in that Gottlieb quote was another thing that writers still expect, but which hasn't happened for most writers since the 1990s:

The quality of our design and production was a further attraction.

Part of that design and production was coming up with a brand identity for each writer published by Knopf. Each writer's books had a distinctive look, which also fit into Knopf's brand identity. (Please look at the chapter on brand identity so you can see how this works.)

In those days, when a writer got picked up by another publishing house, the new publisher usually purchased the entire backlist from the previous publisher, and rebranded.

In short, the branding was done by the publisher.

By the time I came into the business as a novelist, in 1991, this trend was slowly dying. So whenever a writer switched publishers, her brand identity ceased to exist. Some publishers tried to create an illusory brand identity—such as pretend that all of the previous books still mired at other publishing houses did not exist—but readers rarely fell for that.

Writers who got their start in traditional publishing after 1990 or so have no consistent brand identity. None. Only a handful remain lucky enough to have stayed with the same publisher during that time, and those writers might have a consistent brand identity.

I say might because the publishers kept merging, and new editors and new managers came on board, and often the old designs —the old branding—got tossed as newer people took over the publishing house (often to get laid off four or five years later).

Traditional publishing houses no longer have identities. Neither do their writers.

When indie came about, most self-published writers copied what traditional publishers were doing to promote books. And if the traditional publisher was not doing something, writers failed to do it, too.

Some writers had a vague sense that they needed to control their brand identity, and those writers did consistent work on their book covers or their series.

This is where that myth comes from—the one that says the only way to be successful is to write in a series. Everyone knows that a series should have consistent branding, and so series are instantly recognizable. They're easier to market, because they're easier to identify.

If you're a writer like me, though, or like Stephen King or Joyce Carol Oates or any one of a dozen other writers, you don't like playing in the same sandbox each and every day. Your published works are all over the map.

Most writers act like traditional publishers in that instance, and throw up their hands (after eating them first—okay, I hate that phrase, but it's appropriate here). Publishers believe it's impossible to market a writer who writes in multiple genres, with multiple voices, and multiple tones. And because publishers believe it, writers believe it, too.

But it's not impossible to market a multi-genre writer. Fifty and sixty years ago, publishers used to market writers who wrote all kinds of things.

It's all about branding—both identity and image.

So let's talk about brand image now.

Brand Image

The definition of Brand Image from BusinessDictionary.com:[23]

The impression in the consumers' mind of a brand's total personality (real and imaginary qualities and shortcomings). Brand image is developed over time through advertising campaigns with a consistent theme, and is authenticated through the consumers' direct experience.

Okay. There's a lot to unpack in those two short sentences. We'll leave the most fascinating phrase, "a brand's total personality," until last.

But I know some of you read the definition and immediately panicked. *Advertising campaigns?* you thought. *I can't afford an advertising campaign.*

Ignore the word "campaign," and go back to the chapter I did titled, "How To Build A Brand." In it, I explained how branding is advertising, and how you can build a brand slowly. (If you need more ideas, pick up my book *Discoverability* or look at the free [but out of order] posts online.)

The key word in the front part of that sentence isn't "advertising." It's "consistent." Remember, we discussed consistency. In short, write the best books you can (of any genre), and then be consistent in your presentation. Everything from your logo to your typeface to your actual paid advertising (if you have any), even if that advertising is just Facebook ads, make sure you're presenting the same message in similar ways.

Consistency is primarily about quality, though. And the quality is defined by you, whatever you do best. We'll have more on that in future posts, and if this isn't clear, then pick up a copy of *Discoverability*.

The other important phrase in that sentence? "Developed over time." You can't do this fast. No matter how much you want to.

We can't ignore the fact that your brand image is "authenticated through the consumers' direct experience." How many times have you purchased a product only to discover it wasn't as advertised? Sometimes it's better than advertised. And sometimes, it's not as good at all. I can't eat dairy any more. I was happy to discover some vegan cheese that's amazingly good, but so far, I've not been able to replicate pizza, no matter what all the advertising says. (And I'm sorry, chewy and sweet is not what I think of when I think of pizza.)

So you can tell your customers—readers, in our case—that you're giving them the best book they've ever read, but all they'll do is compare your book to all the other books they've read, and you'll probably come up lacking.

Readers make up their own minds about good and bad. What they like about your work might not be what you think at all. So, if you advertise your romantic suspense novel with a bit of humor as chick lit, the chick lit fans will probably hate the book—because your branding, once authenticated by the customer's direct experience, came up lacking.

So, what was brand image for writers before the indie revolution?

It was entirely predicated on the writer's name. J. K. Rowling was quite aware of this when she wanted to write downbeat mysteries. She knew her name was associated with a certain wizard and a certain tone. Her mysteries are nothing like that. So, she tried a secret pen name. Even once she was outed as Robert Galbraith, she kept the name, because that's a signal to readers that the Galbraith books are significantly different than the Harry Potter books.

It's good news for writers that our brand is tied to our names—even now. Because that way, readers will know what they're getting, just by seeing your byline.

Sometimes that expectation is fairly narrow (Harry Potter for J. K. Rowling), and sometimes it's quite wide (all kinds of mystery/suspense/horror/literary genres and subgenres for Stephen King). The consistency isn't necessarily in the genre of the book or even in its characters. It's in the way the writer writes—the way the writer thinks. (More on that in later chapters.)

So...if you've been publishing for quite a while, like most of us who started in traditional publishing, you have a brand image. It might be small, known only to a handful of readers, but their experience with your work gives them an opinion about what you do.

Please note that sometimes the experience they have with your work is like my experience with *The Walking Dead*. I know the TV show exists. I know lots of people love it. I also know I will never, ever, ever watch it, no matter how many times someone implores me to do so.

That brand image is both a positive and a negative thing. I have judged *The Walking Dead* and determined it's not for me, based on reviews, advertising, clips, and the conversations of my friends. I won't sample it any further. My perception of the show (true or not) is that it is not Kris-worthy, so I'm avoiding it.

Those of you who are just starting out have no brand image. None. You haven't published anything yet. Or maybe you haven't published enough. One novel does not a brand make.

So let's finally get to that phrase "brand personality."

A brand is an entity, something that exists by itself.

Gottlieb discusses that in the paragraph from *Avid Reader*. There was a perception of Knopf that was separate from everyone who worked there, separate from the building and the actual list. It was a perception that anything with the Borzoi colophon on it was a quality book—whether that was true or not.

Here's the ironic part: even if a reader didn't believe a book published by Knopf was a quality read, the reader didn't blame Knopf. The reader either blamed himself for not understanding what made the book quality or the reader would say something like, "Well, that wasn't up to Knopf's usual standards."

Not that the book itself was bad or unworthy of being published.

Back in the 1960s and 1970s, it would have taken a whole mess of really bad books to convince readers that Knopf was not a high-quality publisher. It would have to take a lot of evidence to show that Knopf was in decline. The house published Nobel and Pulitzer winners in higher numbers than other publishing houses. It also won a lot more of the literary awards other than the bigs. The decline would have had to have been across the board—in reviews, in awards, and in the loss of the really big "quality" writer names before people stopped associating Knopf with quality.

You'll note that this has happened in the past twenty years. Most of you have never heard of Knopf.

The word "personality" should be heartening to you. Because if the writer is her own brand, then the writer's personality becomes an essential part of the brand.

A writer personality is just like a human personality. Wait! It is a human's personality. With all of its quirks and foibles, with its sense of humor and its vitriolic anger. Readers who like a writer (as opposed to a series) expect to see different sides of that writer, just like you expect to see different sides to your friends.

Determining Your Brand Image

Sometimes it's pretty obvious. Newbies have no brand image at all. None. Zero, zip, zilch. No one has heard of you, so you can build from scratch.

If you're a famous writer, you'll see your brand image reflected back to you in the media coverage, reviews, and—if you're traditionally published—in the way your publisher blurbs your books.

If you're a midlist writer or if you're indie or hybrid, you probably have no idea what your brand image is. Amazon reviews aren't helpful, and you won't have media coverage.

At this point, early on in your branding adventures, I would say that you should ignore your brand image. In other words, follow your parents' advice: stop worrying about what everyone thinks of you.

Just do your own thing.

Part of your own thing, though, is developing your brand identity, which we talked about earlier. If you follow the steps in the chapter on brand identity, and if you are consistent about it, you'll be able to control some aspects of your brand image.

Big Business and Brand Image

Big businesses (not publishing) often hire polling companies to determine what a product's brand image is. The polling company does double-blind tests, comparing one product with the business's product, to determine what the consumer thinks.

Unless you're a truly rich writer, you can't afford to do this kind of work, nor should you.

Polling your newsletter subscribers won't help you here. They're a self-selected group of people who like your work. Your brand image includes people who like your work, people who avoid your work, and people who hate your work. Ironically, the same attributes probably govern all three responses.

The only time that brand image should matter to you at this early stage of building your brand is when your brand image goes seriously awry. By seriously awry, I mean things like Chipotle's E-coli problem a few years ago. They were known for fresh ingredients without preservatives, and some of the coverage of the E-coli incidents said that the lack of preservatives caused the E-coli problem.

Chipotle has been doing serious damage control ever since, working very hard to rebuild and repair its brand. Coke did the same kind of rebuild more than thirty years ago now. Some genius came into Coke headquarters and decided to get rid of the signature product, replacing it with another product. That lasted less than a year, and Coke spent nearly a decade rebuilding its brand image. (That's where the phrase Coke Classic came in. Once upon a time, that was what Coke was, and nothing more.)

Writers rarely need that kind of damage control. When they do, it's for something truly serious.

Janet Dailey plagiarized Nora Roberts. (Dailey was having issues in her personal life, and couldn't meet her deadlines, so she tried stealing instead.) Dailey kept her career, thanks to the intervention of one editor who had championed her from the beginning, but Dailey's brand is tarnished even now.

George R. R. Martin is on the cusp of something serious as well. Every year that goes by without a new book in his fantasy series tarnishes his reputation even more. Much of the large fan base he was building has peeled off in disgust. Will they return when (if) he publishes the next book? Probably not all of them.

Is this a serious enough problem for him to worry about? I don't know. I would be worried about it. But I'm a different kind of writer, with a different personality. The same kind of pressures (the whole world is waiting breathlessly for your next work) nearly sank J. K. Rowling, but she managed to get through it. Whether George does remains to be seen.

If you are lucky enough to know aspects of your brand image, you can play to that image in marketing. Use the positive—and the negative—to attract readers. Sometimes going straight into the face of the negative gets the attention you want for marketing.

As an example, let me use my antipathy to *The Walking Dead*. If I were designing an ad campaign for the TV series, I'd do a lot of what the series is doing now—all the positive reviews, all the great comments, all the surprises. But I'd also have one series of ads that would say something like this:

> *Think* The Walking Dead *is all about the zombie apocalypse? Zombies, zombies, zombies all the time? Then you're missing one of the best shows on television about hope, forgiveness, sacrifice, and what it really means to be human. Zombies—they're just a metaphor. Except when they devour your brain...*

That might bring in a few viewers who didn't realize the show has depth.

The Important Difference Between Brand Image and Brand Identity

Brand image is all about the past. Brand image is what people have experienced with your brand. Past tense. You hear it all the time when folks discuss Stephen King. They think he's a horror writer. That's still his brand image to some people. But he's much more than that.

They have no idea what he has written in the last twenty years.

Brand image looks backward.

Brand identity looks forward. Brand identity is all about the future. You build a brand identity. You can change it, too. Slowly, of course. You can rebuild your brand identity—and if you do it right, you'll eventually change your brand image to something that comes closer to what you want it to.

The biggest difference between brand identity and brand image, though, is control. You control your brand identity. You'll never completely control your brand image.

I find those concepts freeing. I would rather be working toward the future than struggling to control the past.

That's why I tell you to write the next book.

When you try to figure out what your fans "want," or what they expect, you're looking backwards. You're saying, What did I do right and how do I do it again? rather than remembering the passion that brought you to writing in the first place.

What you did right, back then, was write without thought to your "fan base" at all. Write the next book, finish it, market it while you're writing the next book, and stop obsessing about what other people think.

Your brand image will take care of itself, particularly as you learn how to market your current projects.

Worry only about your brand image if something goes seriously, horribly wrong. And let me reassure you here—most writers never have a Janet Dailey level problem in their career. The chances of you suffering through a horrible, serious wrong are pretty slim. You're not going to have fiction contaminated with E-coli.

If you're savvy enough to understand your brand image, use that. If you're not able to see what your brand image is, ignore it.

The real key? Stop worrying about it.

Write the next book. Be consistent in your branding. Market as best you can.

Any time you get stuck in the past, you're making a mistake.

Writing is all about the future.

Keep looking ahead, and you'll be just fine.

"Speaking of consumers, I would like to introduce our new VP of Loyalty."

BRAND LOYALTY

I started this series on branding because of this phrase: brand loyalty. I have been getting frustrated with the advice coming from this year's round of marketing gurus, all of them bent on harassing readers into buying a book.

It took me a while to put my arms around what was bothering me about that, besides the personal. I hate getting nagged. I'm sure you do as well.

I own many different businesses, and three of them are brick-and-mortar retail stores. We built the first of those very slowly, with an eye to repeat customers.

Repeat customers are more than just the people who like what we're doing. Repeat customers are the bread-and-butter of any retail business.

Much as I hate to tell you this, folks, as indie writers, you're in retail. You're selling your books directly to the customer. You might use platforms like Amazon, Kobo, and D2D rather than sell off your website, but you're still providing a product to a customer, just like the book and collectibles stores that Dean and I own are doing.

According to the global management consulting firm, Bain & Company, repeat customers typically spend 67 percent more than first-time customers.[24]

Dean and I have owned retail businesses in the past, before we knew each other and after, and we both learned the value of repeat customers, one satisfied customer at a time. I vividly remember one couple who came to the frame shop and art gallery that I owned in the 1980s. They had my then-husband frame a small but delicate piece of art for them. (My ex was an artist when it came to framing; unfortunately, he left that business.) The couple liked the work so much that they decided to have us frame all of their art. They spent about $3,000 per month, 1980s dollars, until their collection was framed. And whenever they bought new art (which was often), they framed it with us.

No one else spent as much, although others came close. After that couple's first test piece. After they decided they liked us.

When Dean started Pop Culture Collectables, his goal was to get repeat customers. (Mine was to get rid of the collectibles that we no longer wanted.) We live in a tourist town. A lot of people come here and destination-shop once a year at their favorite stores. I'm proud to say that Dean's hard work paid off. A large number of folks make stopping at Pop Culture Collectables (both stores) one of the goals of their trip. (They can get items online, but it's not the same.)

Writers build brand loyalty as well, but until just recently, they had no idea they were doing so. As we discussed in both the brand image and brand identity chapters, writers in the past let the traditional publishers build the writer's brand, and those publishers did a piss-poor job of it.

Publishers tried to make book buying all about them, and what they curated, forgetting—or never really realizing—that in publishing, customer loyalty is brand loyalty...to a particular writer.

I envisioned this particular blog series after I read Targoz

Strategic Marketing's Reading Pulse survey (courtesy of Randy Ellison). Targoz surveyed almost 3,000 people—readers and non-readers alike—about their reading and book buying habits. (Most studies target readers or heavy readers only.) A lot of the information in the survey confirmed what I already assumed, but I hadn't seen any statistics that backed up my assumptions.[25]

The survey also found some data that was just the same as every survey of book buyers: the number one reason people buy a book is because the book was written by one of their favorite authors. When book buyers purchase a book, 60 percent of those buyers do so because the book was written by "a favorite author or an author [they] had read before."

Study after study backs up that particular piece of data. I've cited other studies that have shown something similar in the past. One of those studies came from a now-outdated Romance Writers of America survey commissioned in 2014. (Outdated because much of the survey had to do with format and where books get purchased.) At that point, romance readers told Nielsen (who conducted the survey) that the most important factor in deciding which romance to buy was the story (at #1) and the author (at #2).[26]

A Codex Group survey, conducted about the same time, found that "consumers are willing to pay a 66 percent premium for a book by a favorite author over an unknown author."[27]

Doesn't that 66 percent look familiar? It's almost the same as the Bain & Company percentage referring to repeat customers. Huh. Weird. I wonder why (she types with great sarcasm).

It makes perfect sense, because what those readers are doing is acting like a rational consumer. Consumers all have loyalty to certain brands. We all have loyalties to certain brands. Coke or Pepsi? Ford or Toyota? Apple or Microsoft? Amazon or Everybody Else?

Brand loyalty is the holy grail of marketing. Marketers believe that once a customer becomes loyal to a brand, that customer is hooked for life.

Not entirely true, of course. If the brand messes with its main product, then the customer gets peeved. I no longer buy "clean and pure" Ivory soap, because a decade or so ago, some idiot at the company had to justify their phony-baloney job by adding scent to every bar of Ivory. I had used the soap because I'm allergic to scent. I don't use the soap any more, and like any loyal customer who had to go elsewhere, I'm still peeved about it.

I'm sure you have similar stories about things you loved until someone "improved" them.

Brand loyalty exists partly because the brand provides something important that the consumer is looking for. The other reason that customers become brand loyal is that it makes their decision-making easy.

Behavioral psychologists and behavioral economists disagree ever so slightly on whether or not something called "choice overload" causes consumer fatigue/depression/anxiety, but the one thing they do agree on is this: when faced with a lot of choices, consumers often default to the choice that they're familiar with.[28]

We've all done it: we have five minutes in a bookstore at an airport or the book section of a grocery store, and we need a book right now. We start by looking for a writer/series we love. If we don't find that, we search for a writer we like. If we can't find that, then we try someone new. If you're anything like me in that scenario, you're silently cursing, because you don't have time to find the right book. I often walk out when my five minutes is up with no new purchase at all—and I suspect I'm not alone in that.

Brand loyalty—name loyalty—is something that we writers desire, but it's not something that we can simply will into being. And it certainly doesn't come about by bribing your reader.

Customer loyalty can be bought. In fact, customer loyalty is all about "What have you done for me lately"? According to the Retention Science Blog:[29]

> *Customer loyalty can be encouraged and improved by maintaining overall low prices and offering regular loyalty discounts, special offers or multibuy deals. This will convince your regular customers that you are still the cheapest merchant on the market. In this way it will prevent them from purchasing their products elsewhere.*

Customers are loyal to the price or the deals. Yes, they like the product or the store or the atmosphere, but they can live without all of that if the price is wrong for them.

Brand loyalty is earned. From the same blog:

> *Consumers who are loyal to a brand remain customers because they believe you offer a better service and higher quality than anyone else. This happens regardless of pricing or other financial reasons.*

In fact, the blog points out, that brand-loyal consumers will often try other products marketed under the same brand—even if those products are more expensive than the average product on the market.

Think Apple. Apple's most brand-loyal customers will buy all Apple products, even though they're often the most expensive on the market. Why? It's not just the products, although if the products went downhill, the loyal customers would eventually leave.

It's what CNBC calls "the ecosystem."

Apple integrates its goods and services, and its innovation into a well-designed mesh of stores, apps, and products that make it easy for the customer to move from one service to another. According to CNBC,[30] the "ever-growing, sprawling ecosystem of software and services that allow you to do more with the products if you continue to invest in that ecosystem."

Apple's competitors, for the most part, don't provide a comfortable ecosystem. They're trying to reverse engineer an ecosystem, while Apple had it from the start.

Think about this: the most popular companies in today's business world tend to provide more than a good product at a great price. They provide service, ease of use, adventure, and a way to interact with that system. That's why Amazon is so successful right now. They, too, have an ecosystem.

What has that to do with writers? We don't provide an ecosystem.

Or do we?

People come to us for stories, entertainment, a certain point of view. What they end up liking is our voice and the way we tell our stories. If we entertain them, they come back. If we provide their favorite entertainment, they wait for our next project, whatever that may be. At this stage, they might become an evangelist for our work, letting others know we exist. This is an organic thing, not something you can force, no matter how much you beg.

Then there are hardcore loyalists, who will buy everything we do. Or they might like one aspect of what we do so much they want all of that thing, whatever it is.

Sometimes, they might perceive your work as unique, even when it falls solidly within a genre or a series of archetypes.

I was listening to Joanna Penn's podcast, The Creative Penn, on a break from this blog, and I came across this snippet from Dan Blank on episode 325 that perfectly illustrates what I mean.[31] He said:

I don't really like fantasy books, I don't really like the whole magic and wizard thing, but I love Harry Potter. I'm reading Harry Potter to my six-year-old right now. Again, because Harry Potter to me is not about wizards. It's about friendship, and loyalty, and how you use power, and choices you make in life and all that.

To him, the Harry Potter books are not fantasy novels. They're something other, something greater than fantasy, which is not something he normally reads. (The entire podcast episode is worth your time, especially if you are focused on building your business.)

He is not a consumer of fantasy novels. He is a reader of Harry Potter. And Harry Potter speaks to him.

Which brings us to one other aspect of brand loyalty for writers. Some writers, like me, write in multiple series, formats, and genres. We also write standalones. My most loyal readers like everything I do. Most of my readers segregate my work either by genre or series or length. (Some don't read short fiction, for example; others don't like horror; and some only prefer one of my series.)

There are layers of loyalty to my brand enmeshed in this. I can't guarantee that "my" readers will buy everything I produce. But I know that some will buy everything in the Retrieval Artist series or my Kris Nelscott Smokey Dalton books or my Kristine Grayson novels. So I have separate newsletters for those to inform the readers of those what I'm doing.

The accepted wisdom is that if you write in only one series, then you will be more successful. And to some extent, that is absolutely true. If you hit on the right series, and if that series has certain factors that make it a recognizable brand.

Harry Potter himself is a recognizable brand. J. K. Rowling has also written mysteries that aren't doing as well as the Potter books but which are still wildly successful by most measures.

However, according to that 2014 Codex survey,[32] the author with the strongest brand loyalty is Lee Child. While his books do not sell as well as J. K. Rowling's Harry Potter series or even as well as John Grisham's books, a stunning 70 percent of Child's fans buy his next book. Compare that with Grisham's fans, 41 percent of whom will buy his next book.

There's a significant difference between Child's books and

Grisham's books. Grisham writes many different kinds of books. He writes YA as well as legal thrillers. He writes standalones that are sometimes thrillers, and sometimes straight literary novels. He publishes short story collections. He's written nonfiction at book length.

Lee Child has only written books in the same series about the same character. There's a wide variation in the techniques that Child uses to tell these stories—some are first person; some are third. Some are multi-viewpoint; some are single viewpoint. Some are set in the present; some are set in the past. But they all focus on Reacher, and his response to whatever problem comes his way.

In other words, fans know what they're going to get. They don't have to study the book jacket or read the opening to find out if the book is in a genre that they like. Child minimizes the risk for the buyer by producing very similar products.

It's very smart, and something he did by design. His nearly twenty years of experience in British television taught him how to market a product. It's not fair to say he assembled Jack Reacher, but Child did give thought to building brand loyalty. As someone who worked in television, he knew how to build an audience, which is the first step toward building loyalty.

In a Forbes article by David Vinjamuri titled "The Strongest Brand in Publishing Is...,"[33] Child explains how he thought about getting brand loyalty for his series. I'm not going to quote all of that here because I'd quote a large chunk of the article. So I'm only going to share what I consider to be the most important part of Child's thinking.

He said that the main factor in building brand loyalty is consistency. (He's right, as we discussed in some of the earlier branding chapters.) Here's how he applied that concept to his own writing plans:

A series is better than a sequence of [unrelated] books in terms of building brand loyalty. There are two components of loyalty: one is the author and the second is the subject. If you like the author but you're uncertain of the content of the next book, that's an obstacle. It runs counter to the literary view of writing that values originality and growth. Jack Reacher is the same person in every book.

Child is right about subject matter being an obstacle to a fast purchase. I adore Stephen King, and would count him as one of my favorite writers, but I am not interested in the Dark Tower series. Yet King routinely outsells Child, based on the strength of his imagination and voice.

There's also a danger to consistency as Child applies it here. I was a Jack Reacher fan for about twelve books, but after a while, I grew tired of the very thing that Child calls a virtue here—the fact that Reacher does not change from book to book. I have gone from preordering the next book to not reading the series any longer, because, quite frankly, as a reader, I have become bored.

Do I consider myself a standard reader? Not by any stretch. But I am a fairly standard consumer. I have brands that I like and that I don't want to change (I'm looking at you, Ivory) and brands whose adventuresome spirit I love. I am an Apple user and I love their ecosystem. If they focused on only one product, I'd have moved on by now.

The same with Amazon. Because I live at the ass-end of nowhere, I'm excited to see if the Whole Foods purchase makes it easier for me to get certain kinds of groceries that are simply unavailable here. I trust the Amazon brand to deliver food to me unspoiled, no matter the distance, at a price that I can afford. If Amazon had stuck with books only, like it did twenty years ago, I would not spend as much money with them as I do.

Go back to the earlier chapters. If you are the kind of writer who can write the same thing over and over again and not get bored, then you might be able to develop the kind of brand loyalty that Child is talking about.

I can't. I don't want to repeat myself. So even though I know what he did is very smart, it's not something I can or will replicate. I have to plan my own brand work around that decision.

That said, I am much more interested in building brand loyalty than I am in building customer loyalty. I didn't have the words for this until I started this series.

I don't want people to buy my books because they're discounted or because I keep offering better and better variations of a good deal. I want people to buy my books because they enjoy my books.

My slow-growing newsletter, which is double the size it was last year, gets almost no promotion from me. I want readers to sign up because they're interested, not because I ran some promotion on Twitter.

I'm also aware that a large number of my readers will never sign up for a newsletter, never visit this website, never follow me on Twitter. But they will buy the next book in either a favorite series or in general.

These are the people I'm cultivating. And until 2017, I would have called them fans of my work. I think it's more accurate to say they're brand-loyal customers.

I appreciate them all. My motto is one reader at a time. And do my best to get them to come back to buy more.

How do I do that?

I write the best damn books I can. Everyone's time is precious, including that of readers. They will stop reading an author who no longer entertains them. They will never read an author out of obligation (once they've left school, that is). They all have To Be Read piles that are very high. You want your novels to be one of the books that's actually read, not on the TBR pile.

Remember, folks, writers are the brand here. Your byline is the brand. Not your publisher, not your cover. The name you write under is the brand you are building.

That's important to what comes next.

According to the American Marketing Association, brand loyalty is about the experience a customer has with a brand, not the price the customer pays or what they save.[34]

Remember the ecosystem comments about Apple. Apple provides an all-around experience for its customers. It doesn't just provide a product.

This is a place where writers can excel. More on that below.

Brand Loyalty in General

Let's continue with general brand loyalty for a moment. Here are the things that show up on almost every list of how to get customer loyalty. They are, in no particular order:

1. **Focus on What You Do Best**
2. **Provide Value/Quality**
3. **Be Authentic**
4. **Be Unique**
5. **Make Sure Your Brand is Consistent**
6. **Focus on Customer Service/Make the Consumer Experience Pleasant**
7. **Engage with Your Customers**
8. **Segment and Reward Loyalty Levels**

Or, let's look at it in a different way: brand loyalty is about trust. The consumer trusts the brand to fulfill some need, some promise. One marketer, James Kane, believes that brand loyalty comes about with a "yes" answer to these three questions:[35]

1. *Do you make my life safer?*
2. *Do you make my life easier?*
3. *Do you make my life better?*

Overwhelming and confusing, I know. It's worse if you look at all the websites. A lot of them confuse customer loyalty with brand loyalty, brand image with brand identity, product with company.

I'm going to try to clarify all of this stuff for writers, now.

For the sake of this next section, we're going to consider the writer herself as the brand, not the writer's series. Just the byline.

Brand Loyalty for Writers

Let's start with those three questions, and the word "trust."

To have brand loyalty, the reader needs to trust the writer will provide a great experience. But does that experience make a person's life safer, easier, and better?

Some nonfiction does, automatically. But in this book (and on my blog), we deal with fiction. Does fiction make a reader's life safer, easier, and better?

Absolutely. Fiction gives a reader time to relax, to go elsewhere, to think about other things. In doing so, fiction makes a reader's life easier, and often, by giving just a bit of entertainment, it makes a reader's life better.

Does fiction make a reader's life safer?

Of course. Fiction teaches empathy, for one thing, opens new worlds and new ideas to a reader, and most importantly, makes a reader feel like he's not alone. All of those things—and many more —can make a reader feel safer.

A great author can provide all three to the reader without thinking about it. The writer has no idea how she connects with her readers. The only way she can do so is…

1. Be the Best Writer Possible.

Write at the top of your game with every project. Continue to learn and grow. Try new things. Constantly improve. Become the best storyteller you can. Only write things you're passionate about, and that will make you the best writer you can possibly be.

2. Provide Value/Quality.

Don't put out a half-assed project. Make sure your books are copyedited, your covers are good, and your stories as important to you as possible. Don't write something because someone told you it will sell. Write something because you love it and you want to write about it.

If you write what you love, readers will respond.

3. Be Authentic.

Write what's important to you, not to anyone else. Write from the heart. Even if your writing is in some way flawed, anything that comes from your heart will be one hundred times better than writing that comes from some intellectual "I should write like this because someone told me to" place.

4. Be Unique.

Lee Child dealt with this in the Forbes article I listed above. He said this about the way he created Jack Reacher:[36]

I ignored all the other series. If you start with a laundry list of things then the book won't be organic.

If you want to write something that has been done to death because you love that idea, then write it, but make it yours. If you want to write something that no one else is writing, and you have no idea how to market it (or what it even is), write it, and then figure out how to communicate it to your readers.

5. Be Consistent.

This can mean that you write the same series, genre, or character, if that is what you want to do. But it doesn't mean you have to.

You need to be consistent in the above four points. Your work should always be the best it can be. Make your product branding recognizable—something that screams this is a book by you. (If you'll note, on my novels, the last name Rusch is usually a focal point.)

If you are continually writing what you love, then you will write from a part of you that is uniquely you. That alone will keep your work consistent. Your perspective is yours alone, and impossible to replicate in any way.

Trust the writing process. Trust your work. And trust your readers. They will find what's consistent about your work, even if you can't see it.

6. Make It Easy for Your Readers to Find Your Work.

We writers don't do normal customer service things. We don't have retail stores (or most of us don't, anyway). We market through other retailers. We are introverts, and we don't like spending hours interacting with people. Many writers don't even like social media or blogging online.

So how do writers provide a good customer experience and/or customer service?

Simple. This is actually what we excel at. The good customer experience happens inside the stories we tell, the worlds we create, the entertainment we provide.

Customer service, though, is a different thing. Make it easy for your readers to find another book of yours. Make sure that you have the opening chapter to another novel at the end of your current novel. If you have a newsletter that you use to update your readers on the next project, put that in your books as well.

Have a static website with easily accessible information on the books/series. (This is where I fail, because I built mine wrong—at least under Rusch. For Nelscott and Grayson, and for my Diving and Retrieval Artist series, I do just fine.)

Figure out what questions your readers usually ask, and set up a FAQ so that those questions get answered easily.

And think about this: if you want something from a writer as a reader, chances are your readers want that from you. Provide it, whatever "it" might be.

7. Engage with Your Readers.

This does not mean you have to spend hours on social media or send out weekly newsletters. Nor does it mean you need to answer every question on Wattpad or do an online Q&A.

Figure out how you want to interact with your readers. I give my readers free stuff, but not in the obvious way. I don't put my books on a retail site for free.

Instead, I run a free piece of fiction—in its entirety—every Monday, and have done so every week since 2011. I post a blog for free every Thursday and have done so, except for a six-month hiatus while I finished a big book project, every week since 2009.

I also do a monthly recommended reading list, based on what I read each month. I had stopped doing that for lack of time, but my readers asked me to bring it back. I had thought that no one was reading it, but the moment I stopped, I got letter after letter after letter asking for its return. I now make the recommended reading list one of my major priorities.

Am I constantly writing, talking to, dealing with my readers one-on-one in a public or social media setting? No. But I do give them ways to interact with my work, which is what I care about. I love sharing my stories, my reading choices, and my thoughts on the industry, and people seem to love reading those things.

This is how I chose to engage with my readers, and they seem to enjoy it, if my email and comments are any indication.

You can find a similar way to engage your readers as well. It might be different from mine, but that doesn't matter. What matters is what works best for you.

8. Segment and Reward Loyalty Levels.

I am leaving that language from brand loyalty posts by other people here, because I don't know how to say it better. What the above phrase means is that you reward readers based on their level of engagement.

I provide a lot of free material on this website because, quite frankly, I was really, really, really poor once. I know how important it is for a reader with no money to have access to something good to read. Sometimes those readers end up in better circumstances and will eventually pay to read my work. Most often, though, they won't. But they will be the biggest cheerleaders of my work. They will point out to others that my work is available for free; they will spread word of mouth about the quality of the product, because they're reading it each and every week.

I learned long ago, though, that some people will pay a great deal for something they value. In addition to the free end of the spectrum, it's important to provide the limited edition/expensive end of the spectrum. There are people who love having an exclusive or one-of-a-kind item, and if you can provide it as a writer, do so.

I did a lot more of that years ago, and am coming back to it. The nice thing about that product is that it makes a great giveaway to a loyal reader who cannot afford something that expensive.

Patreon and other platforms provide a different way to segment engagement—people pay for what they want or pay to support whatever they are interested in. Kickstarter has shown that a handful of hardcore fans can fund up everything from movies to music to novels.

You shouldn't just focus on the people who can afford your work. Nor should you focus solely on those who need low, low prices because they're bargain hunters.

Make sure you provide something for everyone. And give those somethings some thought.

9. Develop an Ecosystem.

J. K. Rowling is doing that very well with the Pottermore

website. Pottermore is more than a beautiful website. It's a place to interact with other J. K. Rowling fans, to enter the "wizarding world," to find things to buy, to talk about the books, characters, and ideas in her work. It is an interactive place that brings fans together.

She doesn't run the site personally, but she does oversee it, and it was her idea.

You can do something similar, if you so choose, or you can figure out other ways to create an ecosystem. Sometimes simply releasing story bibles or ephemera or cut scenes will fill this same gap.

The Biggest Key to Brand Loyalty

Acknowledge that you are a brand. Build it one reader at a time. Know that your readers are people, not numbers on your newsletter.

And remember this lovely statistic, courtesy of the Kellogg School of Management at Northwestern University:[37]

Up to 15% of a business's most loyal customers account for 55-70% of its total sales.

It's not how many people buy your books that's important. What's important is how many of those people read and like your books. What's even more important than that is how many of those readers return to your next book, and your next, and your next.

Stop chasing big numbers of downloads or newsletter sign-ups. Start thinking about providing value to your readers.

Then you need to value each reader—even if you only have ten of them. Someday, those ten readers will become twenty, those twenty readers will become 100, those 100 readers will become 1,000.

To put it in retail terms, you want repeat customers. You want to be a destination writer, just like our retail stores in a tiny tourist town are destination stops for people on their annual vacation.

If you think of your readers as people, if you remain grateful for their willingness to spend their hard-earned time and dollars on you, you're on the road to building a brand that will inspire loyalty.

Just remember: one reader at a time.

"After a few false starts I have finally finished
my business marketing plan."

DEFINE YOUR TARGET AUDIENCE: THE INTERMEDIATE STAGES

In the past eight or so years since indie publishing took off, writers found that the commodity they lack the most is time. Time to write. Time to research. Time to read. Time to market.

We get inundated daily with shoulds and have-tos. Someone is always so much more successful than we are, and they're successful at something we've wanted for a long time.

Then there are the overnight sensations, the folks who claim to make $50,000 to $100,000 per month on their writing, even though they have only published five or fewer books. They have some kind of marketing system, and 100,000 people on their newsletter list. They have figured out how to game Amazon's algorithms or they're the first people to use that brand-new marketing tool (cough: Facebook ads) that some gigantic corporation has come up with. Or the first to use it effectively.

They promise: if you only follow these five steps, you, too, can make $50,000 to $100,000 per month on your writing as well.

Only it never works that way. First of all, there's no way to know if the folks who claim to have a working system actually do have a working system. There's also no way to know if that $50,000 to

$100,000 they earned in one month was for just one month or if they consistently earn at that level.

Have they done it for four months? A year? Five years?

Because, I don't know about you, but what I care about in this business is staying in it for the rest of my life. That means building a business, not being an overnight sensation. (Or, becoming, as the music industry so aptly calls it, a "one-hit wonder.")

This book and my blog are geared toward the career writer, not the person who is in it for a fast buck and will leave when the going gets rough. (As many of my readers have noted in my comments and emails, the gurus of 2011 and 2012 have mostly disappeared. Even their websites are down. The ones who have survived have transitioned to career writers and generally don't use gimmicks any more.)

Sure, it would be great to have $100,000 month. You can bet that if I have that kind of spike on five books, I'll be banking the money for a rainy day. I will hope that the money will continue. I will bet that it won't.

Because I have earned that much money in a month off and on throughout my career, and I've learned that what goes up does come down.

The nice thing is, though, if you build your writing career properly, what comes down doesn't come down as far as it had before.

Here's what a proper income spike should look like:

In other words, you have a sales spike, and while you will lose many of those readers, you will keep quite a few of them. You'll end up with more regular readers than you started with. Provided you have a good product that inspires brand loyalty—which is something we dealt with in the previous chapter. Brand loyalty, for writers, is generally to the writer's byline, not to the publishing house or genre or anything else. Sometimes brand loyalty is to a series or a series character. But for the sake of our purposes in this series, think of your author name as the brand, and everything else will fall into place.

When I wrote the initial target audience chapter, I assumed that you either had no idea who your audience actually was or were so new that you had no audience. Today's chapter assumes you have an audience, but you have no idea who they are.

Now, a lot of what I write in these branding chapters takes into account the fact that none of us have any time. Most of us lack the big bucks that major corporations have as well. So doing some of the market research things that marketing and advertising blogs tell you to do to figure out who your audience is are things that we either don't have time to do or the funds to pay someone else to do it.

Besides, how many of you want to send out newsletters or updates to readers, asking them to take marketing surveys? Think about it from a brand perspective. How annoyed would you be if your favorite author wanted all of your personal data so that she could sell to you and people like you better than she already is?

If my favorite author was a nonfiction writer who was a marketing guru and her topics were only about marketing, I probably wouldn't be annoyed. But if my favorite author was a Regency romance writer who had never contacted me before...well, at best, I'd ignore the email. At worst, I'd make a little mental note of my annoyance and do a small compare/contrast: is it still worthwhile to me to buy her books after she annoyed me? Probably yes. But if the annoyance continued…

So how do you find out about the audience you already have? And how do you find out about the audience you might be able to build?

The answer is both simple and hard. You take the information you already have available to you, extrapolate from it, and continue to pay attention to the world around you to gain even more information.

Sounds straightforward. But what does all that mean? What information do you have already? You probably had no idea you have information, except—if you're lucky—emails from readers who liked your work. And please, don't email them back asking them for personal details. Just thank them for taking the time out of their day to make your day a bit brighter.

So, let's find out about your audience by using my audience. (Remember, I'm doing this branding series for myself, to apply the marketing knowledge I have from other businesses to my fiction business. So, I'm multitasking—using what I know to help explain the concepts I'm dealing with here, and educating myself in my own branding at the same time.)

I write two different science fiction series. Right now, I'm deep in my Diving Universe series, a space opera set far from Earth. The stories have a strong female protagonist, a bit of time travel, and lots of action, but also quite a bit of hard sf as well.

How do I find out who my existing audience is?

I look at the also-boughts on Amazon. As I wrote this chapter, I looked in real time at two different books—the first novel in the series, *Diving into the Wreck*, and the third book in the series, *Boneyards*.

The first thing I look at to do audience research is the also-boughts on Amazon and the other e-retailer sites that have also-boughts. Several apps will do this for you. But in the beginning, do it yourself. It helps with your understanding of marketing.

In addition to my own books in the also-boughts (Yay! That means people who liked this book bought other books of mine), I want to know who I share my readers with.

On *Diving into the Wreck*, I find Linda Nagata's brand-new novel (yikes! I need to pick that up), Ann Leckie's newest novel, a writer I've never heard of named Laurence Dahners, John Scalzi, Tanya Huff, Lindsay Buroker, C. J. Cherryh, Sharon Lee, Lois McMaster Bujold, and on and on for another hundred novels or so.

What do these names tell me? They tell me a lot, actually. Here's what I can see just from the names listed.

•I have hardcore sf fans among my readership. They know some classic authors like C. J. Cherryh and Lois McMaster Bujold. They're also up-to-date on the new classic writers, like Ann Leckie.

•My readers buy military sf. Linda Nagata's book is military sf, and farther along in the list, some Mike Shepherd books appear. They're also military sf.

•My readers love space opera. Lois's books are both military sf and space opera, but they lean more toward space opera (in my opinion). C. J.'s are also split between military and space opera, leaning more toward space opera. Ann Leckie's Ancillary Justice series is modern space opera (which is space opera with a touch more hard sf). If you scan through the list, you'll find a lot of space opera in the also-boughts.

•My readers like books with strong female protagonists. The Tanya Huff book covers feature a woman with some kind of futuristic gun (remove the gun, and the covers could work for some of my Diving books).

•My readers like sf with crime in it, as witnessed by the John Scalzi novel on the list.

•My readers like series books. In addition to reading everything in the Diving series, the also-boughts show a lot of repeat names, as readers work their way through other series.

•My readers are adventurous. These also-boughts are all over the sf (and fantasy) map. The books include *New York Times* bestsellers, award-winners, and brand-new indie writers launching their very first series.

I could go on, but I'm not going to.

With the first book in the series, I can see the also-boughts of the people who decided to try the series. But what about the people who are sticking with it? After all, they are my actual audience.

By *Boneyards*, there are a lot more Rusch books in the also-boughts, which pleases me. Linda Nagata reappears right away, as does Lindsay Buroker, Mike Shepherd, Sharon Lee, Tanya Huff, and Lois McMaster Bujold. But some other writers have bumped their way up the list, like Robert J. Sawyer, Yoon Ha Lee, and Elizabeth Moon. Again, lots of books in series, lots of military sf and space opera, less fantasy, and some very hard sf, more than with the first book.

Not a surprise to me, because the Diving series is written in a very challenging fashion—mixing first and third person, past and present tense, time periods all over the map, and a complex backstory.

I'm able to refine, just from that short glance alone, what the Diving readers are looking for. I can't go wrong in assuming that the readers of the Diving series want space opera, a little bit of military sf, and some hard sf as well. They're not afraid to read some challenging works. There's a lot fewer fantasy novels on the list (except for some of mine) as we get to *Boneyards*, so this is a purely sf series.

Let's compare that with my Retrieval Artist series. That's a more mature series—fifteen books long as opposed to six—with a genre mix (detective plus science fiction). I glanced at the first book in the series, *The Disappeared*, and a middle book, *Anniversary Day*.

Some differences between Diving and Retrieval Artist show up almost immediately. Two and a half screens of also-boughts on *The Disappeared* before another name besides mine shows up. Most of those also-boughts are the rest of the Retrieval Artist series. (That happened with Diving, too, but there are fewer books in that series.) Then the Diving series shows up with one book, some fantasy books of mine, and finally...Andy Weir, William Gibson, Elizabeth Moon, that John Scalzi novel again, and a few pages down, Lois yet again.

No military sf at all. Very little space opera. No obviously strong female protagonists. Fewer female sf writers. Harder sf and sf that combines detectives and mystery stories. Some challenging writers who appeal to the hardcore sf reader. A similar audience with crossover, but not the same audience at all.

By *Anniversary Day*, the middle of the series, Andy Weir is nowhere to be seen. A lot more John Scalzi, some Walter Jon Williams, and even Connie Willis has joined the list. Ann Leckie is back as is Linda Nagata. Nathan Lowell is on the list along with James S. A. Corey and David Drake.

A bit of military sf, then, but not much. Space opera, some award-winning writers, even more challenging hard sf works, and a lot of cross-genre mystery works. Fantasy combined with mystery, sf combined with mystery. So the mystery is an attraction but the worldbuilding is as well, since there are no contemporary or historical mysteries in the also-boughts.

That surprises me. I would have thought that mystery readers would have crossed over. But they haven't. Fantasy readers have (also surprising to me) but not mystery readers.

One cannot assume, in doing this work.

Different platforms have different information. I went from Amazon to Kobo to see if they ran also-boughts. They don't call the books listed with mine as also-boughts. They're called "related titles" and they feature an entirely different group of authors and series. (I'm suspecting they are also-boughts, since not all are on-point with genre.)

The names here also give me a lot of information about how Kobo, at least, perceives my audience for these works. If the books listed below are, in fact, also-boughts, then I see how different the international audience is from the U.S. audience.

I could do this all night, and so could you, but suffice to say there's enough information in the also-boughts and related titles surrounding your work to give you the glimmerings of an understanding about your current audience.

But the title of this chapter is your target audience. You want to grow your readership, right? Then you target the readers of the writers on your also-bought list. In the bad old days, you would have had to buy a list or market blatantly (Readers Who Love Lois McMaster Bujold Will Love Kristine Kathryn Rusch!)

You don't have to do that now. If you do paid ads on Amazon, you can target readers who buy books by authors on your also-bought list in your ad buy. You can do the same with Facebook ads and all kinds of other paid advertising that relies on algorithms.

That's just the tip of the iceberg. There are many other things you can do. If you're new or if you're rebranding your series or if you're writing a new series, you can make your covers similar to the covers of the books in your also-bought list. That's why Tanya Huff's book covers could work (with slight modification) for my Diving series—especially the Diving covers done by the original traditional publishing house a long time ago.

Looking at also-boughts is just one technique among a thousand to help you figure out your current audience.

If you know your genre and subgenre, you might be lucky enough to find marketing surveys that list the "average" reader of that genre. The Targoz Reading Pulse survey that started me down this branding road has an entire section on the "average" reader. I got Randy Ellison's permission to share some of that with you throughout this series.

For example, almost all reading and book buying surveys find that women buy more books than men. Some surveys find that women also read more books than men. I'm not sure if that's accurate. The buying more books than men makes sense, because all marketing surveys find that women generally do the purchasing if they're in a committed relationship. That goes for everything from groceries to tools.

There are a million simplistic articles online as to why, including some stupid articles that say women like shiny objects which is why they spend more money. (Seriously!)

But the real reason is more utilitarian. From a 2013 article in Forbes by Bridget Brennan, an expert who spends her entire career studying shopping patterns:[38]

In virtually every society in the world, women have primary care-giving responsibilities for both children and the elderly (and often, just about everybody else in-between). In this primary caregiving role, women find themselves buying on behalf of everyone else in their lives.... If you're in a consumer business, it means that women are multiple markets in one. They are the gateway to everybody else.

Since I know that more women buy more books than men, and I also know that the readers of my Diving series buy a lot of books by women and with women on the cover, I would assume that the majority of my readers are women.

But I don't know that for a fact, and the Reading Pulse survey makes me reconsider my assumption with this little tidbit:[39]

Science Fiction & Fantasy (SFF) is one of the few genre subsets that has a majority male readership (68% male). The average SFF reader is a married 30-year-old (55%), college educated (52%) male who is a moderately active

117

reader (38% read 12 or more books a year, and 35% read 5–11 books a year),
buys a moderate number of books to match (20% buy 12 or more books a year,
and 32% buy 5–11 books a year), and cares about convenience above all else.

A quick mental double-check of the fan mail I've received, a scan of my Twitter followers, and my other social media interactions makes me realize that I have a lot of readers who fall into the demographic listed by the survey.

The survey goes on to show that these readers read a lot of series and tend to buy a lot of ebooks for the convenience. Which leads me to think about the fact that my also-boughts are filled with other books from the same series, and then books from other writers' series, again, backing up some of the information in the survey.

How do I use this? We'll deal with that more in some of the following chapters, but the first way to use it is to leave my assumptions at the door. I'm not just marketing to women when I market sf books. I'm marketing to a largely male audience, who loves books in series.

Does that mean I should stop marketing to women? Heavens, no. But it does mean I should expand my own thinking about marketing my work to include the male readers, maybe more than I already have been.

There are other ways to use this information as well. If and when I plan to rebrand the covers of these series, I might consider a bit more military sf covers for Diving and some more noirish covers for Retrieval Artist. Or see what the current crop of covers for other books are at the time.

I might end up gearing my Diving promotions more toward the space opera crowd, and my Retrieval Artist promotions more toward the mixed mystery and fantastical world crowd. I have choices, now that I understand what the readers like about the series.

I've only used a few pieces of information here to show you about target audience. There's a lot more information out there— such as the marketing studies for movies in the same genre or for similar TV shows (*Star Trek*, *Stargate*, and *The Expanse*, anyone?) All of that becomes useful in dealing with the midrange target audience —the existing audience.

As I said above, we're all pressed for time, and simply using some of these simple tricks will refine your marketing to reflect your target audience. And to grow your audience by appealing to the readers who like similar works.

What you want to do is get those readers to sample your work, but you don't want to give that work away. You want the readers to value your work enough to buy the next book, not wait for another freebie.

How do you do that? There are a million marketing tricks. For example, the first book in the Retrieval Artist series is cheaper than the other books by a significant amount (but still expensive enough that I can occasionally discount the book for a Book Bub or some other promotion).

I have introductory bundles for Diving and the Retrieval Artist so that readers can buy the first three books in both series for less than buying the books individually.

And I often participate in promotions like a Storybundle, which unites writers of similar works. The hope is that readers who are fans of one of us will buy the bundle to get ten books for $15 (and support a charity), and read my book, decide they like my work, and buy more of it.

That's another way to do cross promotion with other authors. It works, too. I noted that on one of my Retrieval Artist books, there was a sprinkling of Rebecca Cantrell's work. That makes sense—she has a series that mixes crime with the fantastic, and that's the work that appeared on the also-bought list.

Good marketing really is a science, but we're writers. We only have time to do so much.

Fortunately, a lot of folks are making data collection easier and easier for us, so that with just a bit of knowledge, we can use newly created tools to our own advantage.

You just have to be willing to spend an afternoon delving into your own readership—without bothering the readers themselves. Their purchasing habits have provided you with enough clues to move forward on your branding and your marketing—without losing too much writing time to all this advertising work.

Don't be intimidated by this. Remember, you can get your marketing wrong—and probably will. But the key isn't to do perfect marketing. The key is to try, maybe fail, try again, maybe succeed, and then keep trying all kinds of things.

However, keep in mind that your most important job is to write the next book. You want to see those also-boughts filled up with your own work, like mine are. Because that means that readers liked what they read and went on to buy the other books you've written. The more books you have for them to find, the more they'll buy. The more they buy, the more likely they are to become regular readers.

And, as I mentioned in the brand loyalty chapter, the regular readers are the ones who become brand loyal. Returning customers are more than 60 percent of every single retail business.

They should be part of yours as well.

Don't forget them in your search for new readers. Remember to acknowledge your faithful readers, because they are the ones who put the food on your table. They're the folks who already form your audience, and they're the ones who deserve your loyalty in return.

How? Well, that's a topic for another chapter.

But do say thank you every now and then. Because you wouldn't be where you are without them.

He had reduced his business strategy
panic attacks to under three hours.

HOW TO BUILD A BRAND: THE INTERMEDIATE STAGES

I'll be honest with you: I struggle with these branding posts. Not because I am unfamiliar with what I'm writing about. I know this topic inside out, upside down and backwards. I've built two publishing companies. I've built retail companies. I've worked in advertising. I've worked for places that were so aware of their brand...that they knew when a topic or a product deviated from that brand in a harmful way.

Unfortunately, the way that traditional publishing was—and is—structured, writers who work in that part of the industry have no control over their brand at all. (I can think of 1.5 exceptions—James Patterson took over his marketing right from the start, so he always controlled his branding; Lee Child also gave branding a lot of thought, but left the actual marketing to the publisher. He's the .5 in the equation here.)

So as I wrote these posts, I felt a deep frustration. Because my brand, in almost all of its forms, is extremely messy. Kristine Kathryn Rusch writes all over the map, but was never marketed as a writer whose focus is diversity (in content as well as in genre). Kris Nelscott's traditional publisher was so frightened of my skin color and my topic that they never ever came up with a consistent cover brand, let alone a marketing plan. Kristine Grayson's two traditional publishers had diametrically opposed marketing plans for the books. (The first one worked; the second one…didn't.)

I'm frustrated because I'm trying to fix something that is badly broken in my own career. Many other writers—once traditional and now hybrid or indie—have the same problem. And God forbid if we have tried different genres or had series abandoned in the middle. Traditional publishing was, in its way, antithetical to any kind of consistent branding, at least for the midlist writer, at least in the past twenty years.

These posts, as I said from the beginning, are for me, writing to myself about all the various things I can do to improve my branding or, in most instances, take control of it.

The simplest way for me to take control of my branding would be to pare down everything I do under Rusch to one series, one subgenre. That's what Lee Child does. If I had his Jack Reacher series, I could easily rebrand it, take over the advertising, take over the brand idea and brand identity, and create something unique.

Believe me, I've thought of that. Not for Rusch, but for Grayson, and for Nelscott. I'm refining those latter two brands a bit.

But I have a hummingbird brain. I alight on different things at different times. I read that way, too. I'm not the person who can do the same thing day after day, year after year for the rest of my life.

If I were in the lucky position that most of you indies are in, I could define my Rusch brand from the beginning as something that spans genres, that uses a multitude of styles, that promises quality of a certain type, but never compromises on some things.

I would make my hummingbird brain—my tendency to mix up genres and styles and moods—a huge part of the branding.

I'll be doing that going forward, of course, but that feels a bit to me like closing the barn door after the horses got out—decades ago. (Hell, in this metaphor, that barn might not even have a door any more. It's toppling, needs paint, and maybe needs to be torn down so we can build a brand-new barn. {sigh}.)

I find the topic overwhelming, never more so than in this particular chapter: How to Build a Brand: The Intermediate Stages. The intermediate stages are, technically, where I am, on everything.

Only the foundation I'm building on—in the marketing side—is wobbly. The foundation—on the writing side—is so solid that you could take a jackhammer to it and you wouldn't even chip the concrete.

This is the point where I remind you that everything we discuss in this book is about marketing, which you should never, ever, ever take into your writing office.

If you write what authentically interests you, you will develop an audience. If you decide that you're going to write Jack Reacher-light because it worked for Lee Child, and that's the only reason you're going to write it (a marketing reason, by the way), then you will fail at developing any kind of audience.

And as we've seen in previous chapters, what you want is a loyal audience, one that returns over and over to your work because they love it, not because your work is cheap or because they're waiting for the next Reacher novel and yours will do in the interim.

So...remember. Everything I'm discussing here is about marketing, not writing.

In the first how to build a brand chapter, I explained a lot of the ideas and terms I'll be using in this chapter. If you haven't read the previous chapter, you should do so now.

In that chapter, I assumed you were building your brand from scratch. Maybe you had a few books or a series or a couple of series, but you had done no marketing, really, and hadn't done anything more than considered branding your covers.

For this chapter, I'm going to assume you've been at the writing game for a while. You did the work from the previous chapter on identifying your existing audience, and now you're going to try to make use of that information somehow.

To review, here are the steps to building a brand, no matter what stage we're discussing:

1. **Define Your Business**
2. **Define Your Target Audience**
3. **Research Similar Businesses**
4. **Figure Out What Makes Your Brand Unique**
5. **Figure Out What Your Brand Is Not**
6. **Create a Brand Mission Statement/Tagline**
7. **Be Consistent**
8. **Be Patient**

Because of what we've been working on, I'm going to assume you've defined your business. I'm also going to assume that you now know who reads your books. (As well as you can know it, without doing expensive market research.)

So, let's move forward, shall we? We're going to use my work as the basis of brand building here, and we're going to do it on my two series that I mentioned in the previous chapters.

Before we get there, though, let me be clear: what I'll be doing on branding the Rusch business incorporates all of my Rusch books and all of my various Rusch series. In 2010 or so, I gave serious consideration to pruning my existing series and work down to one or two items.

I decided against it, not just because of my hummingbird brain, but because of my existing audience. I have readers who read everything I do. I have readers who only read the mystery short stories, readers who only read the fantasy books, readers who only read the time travel stuff—and readers who only read the nonfiction.

If I pared down to my two big science fiction series, I would be losing readers rather than gaining them.

That said, my series themselves are brands, with loyal readers who eagerly anticipate the next book. I'm not going to look at Rusch as the brand here, but at the series as the brand.

Unlike the previous chapter, where I looked at the series separately, here I'll look at them together.

Research Similar Businesses

As I mentioned in the original "How To Build A Brand" post, it's almost impossible to research other writers. We're still in the early stages of writers accepting that they are a business, let alone branding themselves as one.

However, I'm going to assume I did the due diligence on wider business brands—TV, gaming, movies—of a similar type.

Now, we'll deal with similar businesses that my existing readers liked. That means looking at the other series and authors listed in the also-boughts on my books (listed in the previous chapter).

Look at the covers, look at the way those series (or authors) are being branded, see if there are any similarities with your work, and then see if there's anything those other writers/series are doing on marketing that you can do as well.

Mostly, you'll be looking at covers, blurbs, where these writers got reviewed, whether or not they advertise on websites or do Facebook marketing, that sort of thing. Is the first book in the series lower priced? Is there a hook that seems similar?

A lot of that research factored into the previous chapter. I learned about the readers and what they're interested in from the also-boughts, and showed you how to do the same. (There are other ways to go about it as well—market surveys, surveys that the film and TV studios do, demographic information in *Ad Week* and other places that will also help you research, if you're so inclined. There are many online tools that will help you as well. Because those tools change daily [it seems], I'm not going to list them here.)

Figure Out What Makes Your Brand Unique

In your research (above), you're looking for similarities. But while you use those similarities for things like keywords and Amazon ads, you also need to know how to separate your work from the works in the also-boughts.

What makes your series/work different from those others?

In the case of my Diving series, a lot of the also-boughts are space opera or military sf (or both), but very few of them have time travel, and even fewer have the rather literary writing style that (for some reason) my brain keeps insisting belongs in this series. Also, the Diving series continues to win readers awards and also exists in shorter formats (short stories, novellas). While most of the series that are in the also-boughts started as shorter works, almost none of them have produced shorter works in the series once the series started.

How I'd use that, besides helping with the newsletter or Free Fiction Monday, I have no idea. But I'm sure I can come up with something.

As for the Retrieval Artist, most of the sf detective series follow the same-old, same-old plotline—detective encounters something weird, detective explores the something weird, detective solves the something weird.

The Retrieval Artist series, from the start, has been modeled on Ed McBain's 87th Precinct series, as well as Elizabeth George's Inspector Lynley series (which is incorrectly named). Both series feature multiple characters and often focus on one of the side characters without exploring the main character.

Unlike those two mystery series, though, I decided (for some reason) to try every subgenre of mystery in the Retrieval Artist series—from cozy to police procedural to locked room to thriller. The *Anniversary Day* saga was supposed to be one standalone thriller novel. Hah! Fooled me. Because I was dealing with sf, I couldn't use shorthand to explain anything, so the single book became three, then became six. And that's worth marketing all on its own.

There are a lot of similarities to the other series/works on those also-boughts, but there are a lot of differences as well.

When you go through yours, make two lists—one of similarities and one of differences. You'll be surprised at the things you'll dig up.

Figure Out What Your Brand Is Not

In doing the work of discovering similarities and differences, you'll figure out what your brand is not. You'll actually see it pretty clearly.

The also-boughts confirmed what I already knew about the Retrieval Artist series. It's not military sf by any stretch. Sometimes it's not space opera either. Even though it doesn't have the literary stylistic tricks that Diving has, the Retrieval Artist series falls into the very center of the sf genre, which is why writers as diverse as Robert J. Sawyer and Connie Willis are on the also-bought list.

Even though I think of Diving as hard sf, the readers don't. The hard sf writers/series in my also-boughts are writers like Linda Nagata, who writes hard sf, but with a military slant. Mentioning the core of the sf field is probably a lot less important to the Diving readership than it is for Retrieval Artist.

Some of the things that the books are not seem obvious to me, but wouldn't to readers. While Diving is adventure fiction, it is more Christopher Nolan than *Pirates of the Caribbean.*

The Retrieval Artist books are more mystery than sf, even though they wouldn't exist without their sf setting. The Retrieval Artist books always do what mystery novels do—they put order on chaos. Whatever the major problem is in those books, that problem gets resolved by the end.

But, because mystery readers are loathe to cross to sf, marketing to pure mystery readers is not what I should do in the intermediate stage here. Because, as the also-boughts show, pure mystery readers aren't crossing over.

However, readers who like mystery in their sf and fantasy are crossing over, so more of the marketing should focus on them.

Create a Brand Mission Statement/Tagline

I resist doing that for each series because of who I am. It limits me creatively as a writer.

But as a writer brand—Rusch—the mission statement/tagline is something like "All genres all the time." Or "expect something different." Or something along those lines.

Of course, I haven't been able to develop that organically from the beginning of my writing career (like so many of you indies can), so I'm reverse engineering this part.

As I was researching this part of the chapter, I did find two cool mission statements for existing brands. I had forgotten all about Apple's mission statement, which also served as its tagline for years: *Think different.* Which continues to define what they do. They're not just a tech company. They're constantly trying to change how we live our lives. Trying to be different.

The other cool mission statement that I found comes from Nike. Their advertising tagline is *Just Do It*, which, quite honestly, I love. I find it inspirational in a good way.

But that's not their mission statement. Their mission statement is this: *To bring inspiration and innovation to every athlete in the world.*

You see it in their products. Their product lines run from the person who walks to work and doesn't put out much effort to the elite athletes who sign endorsement deals with them.

That statement informs everything they do.

Which is why I'm really clear about Rusch. My mission statement for Rusch is my mission statement for life. I need to challenge myself constantly, trying new things, experimenting and growing. That's who I am as a person and as an artist.

The mission statement for Grayson is easier: *It's Not Easy To Have A Fairy Tale Ending*. Grayson will always be goofy paranormal with a touch of romance, usually focusing on myths and fairy tales.

And for Kris Nelscott—realistic hard-boiled fiction from the not-so-distant past. That's not a great mission statement because I haven't refined it. But the Nelscott books deal with the search for justice in a world filled with injustice. I'm so certain of that brand that even though I set some stories in the 1960s and 1970s, I can tell you if they're a Rusch story or a Nelscott story from the theme.

Nelscott is not quite noir because my protagonists get justice in every book. They don't necessarily do so legally, however. But they do "win," and they do their best to be heroes, even in a world that doesn't accept them as such.

Have fun figuring out your mission statement. And realize that it might change down the road as your view of your own art changes.

Be Consistent

I pretty much said what I needed to in the first chapter about Building a Brand. Just because you now know who is reading your books doesn't mean you should change anything. In fact, you're building just fine with what you're already doing. Just keep doing it.

If you want to see consistency on a smaller level—the cover level —look at Allyson Longueira's blog on WMG Publishing's website. She examines how she, as an award-winning graphic designer, thinks when she establishes the cover branding for a series of books. She uses art and examples. Take a look.[40]

Be Patient

You're still learning and growing as a business person. You may not get a lot of result from your branding...yet. What you're trying to build is brand loyalty, and that takes years.

Inc.'s website has a good short article from 2013 about building a brand.[41] The article emphasizes that it's not the external features of the brand that are important, but how the brand makes the consumer feel. Does the brand give the consumer a positive feeling (as in *Oh! I love the last book. I want this new one*)? That's the ideal.

What I love about this article, though, is this analogy:

Your brand is like a bank account. When you delight customers, it adds value to the brand. If you have a string of great products, customers will forget the occasional flop. Apple is a case in point. Few people remember that they've had some real stinkers.

Similarly, when you irritate customers, it extracts value from the brand, and eventually you end up overdrawn and even if you change your ways and come out with some great products, it may take years, if ever, for customers to forget the taint.

Building a brand happens slowly, one product at a time, one interaction at a time, one customer at a time. You can't force a quick reaction. In fact, if you try, you'll probably make a bad impression.

Think of all the complaints that readers are making about that sharing of newsletter lists among writers. That's making a bad impression, just like constantly haranguing your readers to buy, buy, buy your same five products is also making a bad impression. The brand then becomes associated with something bad, not something good.

Character Matters

There's still a lot of marketing psychobabble here, stuff that makes most writers run and hide. I found the perfect way to think about a brand for writers, though, in an article called "How To Build

A Brand From Scratch" by Seattle marketing firm Audience Bloom.[42]

The post's author Jayson DeMers has this lovely analogy right smack in the middle of the article:

> *Instead of thinking of your brand in the colorless term of a "corporate identity," instead, think of your brand as a human being—a fictional character. What would this person be like in real life? How would they talk? What would they look like? How would they dress, walk, and act in different situations? Can you see this person making a good impression with your target demographics? Why or why not? Make adjustments accordingly, and sculpt your character as you would for a character in film or literature.*

He then points out that, for years, Apple used this very concept in its Apple versus PC ads featuring Justin Long and John Hodgman. Those ads were memorable and spot-on in the way both brands were perceived at the time.

You folks do character sketches all the time. This is in your wheelhouse. So give that little exercise a try.

Finally...

In this intermediate stage, you're still refining your brand. You haven't finished building yet. (You'll never finish building, but you will be able to slow down on construction at some point.)

Give it time. You don't have to do all of this at once.

Remember, the best thing you can do is produce the best product ever. Write the next book. And the next book. And the next book.

Yes, marketing is important. But you're a writer, not a marketer. You will be building a brand just by publishing more than one book.

Go slow, be patient, and remember that you're in this business for the long haul.

The most important things you can do? Write and publish. Devote 90 percent of your time to those things. Then focus on the marketing for the remaining 10 percent. As you do, think about building a brand. Think about adding to that brand bank account.

Do one or two things, then go back to writing.

And have fun!

HOW TO EXPAND YOUR TARGET AUDIENCE: CHOICES

The next three chapters about target audience came about because my blog readers asked how to define your target audience. In the first How to Build a Brand chapter, I listed eight steps to building a brand. Step 2 was Define Your Target Audience. I then explained what I meant by that in 400 words—and thought that was sufficient.

Defining, building, and expanding a target audience is as natural as breathing for me. But not for most writers. Most don't have business experience, and apparently most have not worked in companies that jealously guard their brand and their image. So most writers have not learned how to operate in a business world that includes an audience.

And by that, I mean, consumers.

I'm not saying readers, because not everyone reads. But most people buy books—even if those people don't read. That's why I found the Targoz Reading Pulse survey that started this entire branding series so valuable. Targoz talked to readers and non-readers about their book buying habits.

Why are non-readers buying books? Because they have friends, family, and loved ones who read. A lot. So if the non-reader wants to give the reader a special gift, the non-reader buys a book.

Everyone buys a book at one point or another. Most people buy at least one book in a year.

But that doesn't mean that people buy just any book. And that also doesn't mean that when you start thinking about expanding your target audience, you will be able to expand that audience to include all book buyers.

Yet this is where writers start. When they think they need to define their target audience, writers immediately jump to "How do I get everyone to buy my book?" More savvy writers jump to "How do I get all fantasy readers to buy my fantasy novel?"

Neither of those approaches is very helpful, and most turn away more readers than they appeal to.

The reason I initially divided the target audience posts into three was because there really are three steps toward building an audience.

1. **You must acquire an audience.**
2. **You must recognize that you have an audience—a very specific audience.**
3. **You might decide to expand that audience.**

Please read the previous two chapters on this subject before you read this one. I want to make sure we're on the same page here.

For the sake of this chapter, I'm going to assume you have done the homework from the second target audience chapter. You now have an idea as to who reads your work. (The enterprising among you might actually have more than an idea. You might have actual numbers.)

Most writers—most businesses, in fact—believe that the next step is to actively grow that audience. And that belief is a mistake.

In your writing business, as in all business, there is no one-size-fits-all model. That goes to everything from building a business to building a brand. Even if you're in the same field as someone else, your business is different. What you do with that business is based entirely on your goals for that business.

Um, what? you might ask.

Yep, expanding an audience fits into your business goals, not just into branding. Change happens all the time in business, but growth happens only when a business actively pursues that growth.

You'd think that businesses would want to grow, but rapid growth can be harmful to a business. When Dean and I started Pulphouse Publishing, we had planned for slow growth only, and instead, we had exponential growth. It caught us flat-footed. We had not planned in any way for exponential growth—not in staff, or production, or expenses. We started behind, and never really caught up.

Writers who experience rapid growth, especially early in their careers, rarely make it past the first five novels. The writer expects the next books to do as well as the first. Sometimes the sophomore effort does better, but rarely. And by the fifth book, the writer is so deep in their head that they're no longer having fun with the writing itself.

I'm watching that with dozens of successful indies, who are always chasing the same numbers they had on previous books or in previous months, instead of banking the money and going back to having fun with the writing. The fact that the writer had fun with the writing is why the first book (or books) did so well in the first place.

This is why, throughout the entire book, I'm telling you that the things I'm discussing apply only after the writing is over. Never take these principles into your writing office.

The writers who do take these principles into their writing office often end up writing a genre they hate or forcing themselves to write the same type of book over and over again, even if it bores them.

And the marketing-heavy writers, the ones who became successful because they had some marketing gimmick, realize within a year or so that the gimmick no longer works for them. Either the writer must come up with a new gimmick or they need to plant butt in chair and start writing again.

Most writers, though, are not heavy marketers. Most want to ignore marketing altogether. While that's no longer possible in today's indie world, writers can plan a marketing day each week or a marketing weekend every few weeks to focus on what they want.

Once the writer has figured out who their readers actually are, then the writer needs to figure out if they want to grow their audience.

Or, let me rephrase that, the writer must choose whether to focus on growing their audience slowly or aggressively. Or ignore the idea of growing the audience at all.

Strategy One: Ignoring Growth

From the beginning of the modern publishing era, writers left growing the audience to their traditional publishers. That left most writers hard-wired to ignore growing an audience. Writers figure that the audience will take care of itself.

If you do the elementary things we talked about earlier in this series, branding to series, good covers, good blurbs, and (most importantly) writing great and compelling books, then some growth will happen, even without any action on the writer's part.

Eventually, however, that growth will stop. The writer's audience will actually decline. The decline comes from attrition or from inattention or both. Readers die, have life events that make them stop reading for a while, or they actually forget the name of the writer and miss the next book.

Or the genre moves, or gets glutted, or changes labels. Urban fantasy was once part of contemporary fantasy. Then urban fantasy became its own subgenre. And then urban fantasy outgrew contemporary fantasy, and became a genre in and of itself.

If an indie writer ignored those developments, leaving the covers and blurbs (and key words) the way they were for the contemporary fantasy market, the audience would no longer find the books. The audience would fade away, because the writer had stopped doing basic marketing—had stopped paying attention.

However, the ignoring-growth strategy will work for years at a time. Think of it as plateaus. A writer focuses on growing her audience for a year, then manages to grow the audience. She turns her attention to writing a group of books, has a marketing plan for them, and puts them out, without looking at growing the audience at all.

Three years later, she realizes her audience has plateaued, so she focuses on growing the audience again. She's successful: the audience grows. She then lets the audience plateau while she focuses on the writing again.

And so on and so forth.

The strategy is pretty simple:

1. **Focus on your core business.**
2. **Grow your reach.**
3. **Focus on your core business again.**
4. **Grow your reach again.**

And so on, as long as you would like to do that.

It's a strategy that includes ignoring the growth for a while, and believe me it works. I do it for a different series all the time. I focus on them, then I move to a different series, and focus on it for a while.

However, you need to choose to do this. You can't just close your eyes and walk through this modern marketing world. If you're going to ignore audience growth for a while, plan it, and then come back to it. Otherwise, your audience will decrease rather than increase.

Ignoring growth is a short-term strategy. It does not work in the long term. For the health of your business over years, you must grow your audience and your reach.

For example, if your subgenre gets glutted, and you haven't grown beyond your core audience, some of that audience will peel away because they're tired of the same-old same-old. If you have slowly grown your audience over years, you can afford to lose some of those people.

You won't make as much money, and your sales will go down.

Don't panic. Start figuring out how to grow your audience again.

And no, I don't mean write in a different subgenre (unless that interests you). Figure out how to market to the readers who've gotten tired of the same old branding, the same old blurbs, the same old sexy vampires (okay, that's just what I'm tired of. Nothing to see here. Move along).

Refresh your brand—or find people who haven't yet entered this market, and get them to read your book. You can do it.

Savvy companies refresh brands all the time, bringing in people who would once vow they never want to read about another sexy vampire again.

Strategy Two: Slow Growth

Most writers chose to slow-grow their audiences. Most publishers who actually know business and marketing do the same.

Growing an audience slowly makes sense in the way the industry works now.

Due to a lack of shelf space decades ago, publishers worried about growing a writer's audience only when a new book came out —and only for a few weeks at that. Readers had to be aware of that book in those few weeks and buy that book then, or the book would vanish.

Now, though, there's no reason to buy a book until the reader is ready to actually read that book. Rather than subjecting readers to a fire hose of Buy! Buy! Buy!, the writer can make readers aware of the writer's works bit by bit.

Slow growth means doing a promotion for Book #1 one week, doing something to bring attention to the writer himself a few weeks later, doing a promotion for Book #5 a month after that. The attempts to grow the audience reach out to different groups with a different product at different times.

Rather than acquiring thousands of potential readers in a six-week period of time, the writer gains new readers by the handful— ten here, a hundred there, five later on, fifty in a month or so. Over time, those handfuls add up.

The audience doesn't grow by leaps and bounds. Instead, the audience accrues, going from an anthill to an actual hill so slowly that the writer might not even notice the growth until she looks back a few years and realizes that her book sales were one-fifth what they are today.

This strategy is a bit more complex than Strategy One. For Strategy Two, the writer actually needs a marketing plan, with ideas on ways to grow the audience bit by bit.

Strategy Three: Aggressive Growth

Most of the strategies for writers to grow their readership that come from so-called marketing gurus are actually aggressive-growth plans that these gurus stumbled upon. Aggressive-growth strategies rarely work for the long-term.

Businesses that attempt aggressive growth usually have a reason for doing so—and that reason is not getting their product in the hands of millions rather than thousands.

There's usually a business reason for doing it quick and dirty, because quick and dirty can hurt the brand if done incorrectly.

Aggressive growth strategies require a huge investment—usually of time or money or, most often, both. Done correctly, an aggressive-growth strategy can increase a brand's audience by five to ten percent, but rarely more than that.

Aggressive-growth strategies also require constant nurturing. Businesses can't do the same thing over and over again. There will be diminishing returns. So any business attempting aggressive growth needs a rotating plan of ways to promote to a variety of different markets in a variety of different ways with a set purpose in mind.

The most effective aggressive-growth strategies have a large data focus. They require the company to try something huge and expensive (in time or money). While that huge and expensive something is ongoing, the company rakes in data, judging whether or not the huge and expensive something is actually worthwhile.

If the huge and expensive something doesn't move the growth needle at all, then that particular huge and expensive something gets abandoned.

The company then moves to the next thing on the list. Yes, that thing too is huge and expensive, but it's completely different. The company tries that second huge and expensive something, doing the same data analysis, until the company succeeds at getting what it wants from its aggressive-growth campaign—or until the company runs out of time and/or money to run an aggressive-growth campaign.

If a slow growth strategy is complicated, an aggressive-growth strategy is complicated on steroids.

Personally, I would love to see a writer-business do a proper aggressive-growth strategy, pulling in big marketing firms and big data. I'd love to know what works or doesn't work.

But we're talking about a sustained three- to six-month campaign in which the company invests hundreds of thousands of dollars and thousands of hours of work time. To my knowledge, no traditional U.S. publishing company has done this in the 21st century. I know of a few that did this kind of marketing work in the early 1960s, essentially inventing book marketing as traditional publishers do it now, by finding what works and what doesn't work.

For your indie business, an aggressive campaign to grow your audience would require you to do the opposite of Strategy One. Rather than focusing on writing, you would focus on marketing 24/7, and write only when necessary to add to the product base.

All of you have heard of writer-marketing gurus who do that. They go on blogs and talk about their marketing strategies, then mention that they need to take a month "off" to write the next book.

Strategy Four: The Combination

The combination strategy combines ignoring your growth with aggressive growth. You write for a few years, then market aggressively for a year or so, then go back to writing. Or compress the timeline— write for six months, aggressively market when the new book is done, then ignore marketing for another six months and write the next book.

It sounds good, but you'd have to be a good marketer and a good writer to pull this off. Most writers are good at writing, but not at marketing. And most marketers are good at marketing, but not all that great at writing.

It's rare to find both in the same individual. Of course, if the writer has a lot of money, then she might want to consider partnering with someone who has a lot of marketing expertise to figure out a new, aggressive, marketing plan that will get that writer's work in front of thousands of people—without doing the same thing that traditional publishers have done for years.

Details, Please!

By now, you've noticed that I went vague on you with Strategies Two through Four. I did that on purpose.

I realized as I started into this topic, that I could write 400 words on each strategy and get tons of letters from you asking for more explanation, or I could actually devote the kind of time that the topics need.

So the next two chapters will explore growing your audience slowly and growing your audience aggressively. You can figure out on your own how to combine marketing strategies.

Things to remember as we move into the next two chapters—slow growth rarely interferes with building a brand. Most people aren't going to notice if you promote to one group or another, or try to find a new audience and fail.

Aggressive growth risks alienating everyone. Done incorrectly, it can piss off existing customers and drive away new customers. Marketing that focuses on aggressive growth will often result in consumers forming an opinion about the brand without trying the brand, which is antithetical to what you're trying to do.

Your goal is *brand loyalty*—getting readers to return every time you put out a new book. If they form an opinion about you without reading your work, they won't pick up the next book or the next. They might be curious about your work, but they won't be loyal to the brand.

And if that happens, then you'll have to rebuild the trust in your brand—with people who have never even tried it. That requires a whole new marketing strategy, and often one that's subtle and sensitive and the exact opposite of aggressive.

So, your assignment this time is to think of how many brands you have opinions of because they did a massive marketing campaign that bothered you or made you feel like the brand was not for you. Maybe look around your community and see if someone is doing aggressive marketing right now.

Notice who hooked you with a hardcore marketing campaign or figure out if any anyone ever caught your attention with that kind of campaign.

These campaigns and brands should not be books or writers. Everything else is fair game. But remember, the book business has been unbelievably crappy at both branding and at growing an audience, so taking lessons from the book industry is like taking lessons on skydiving from someone who has never gotten into an airplane.

Have fun with this, and I'll see you in the next chapter...when you're ready.

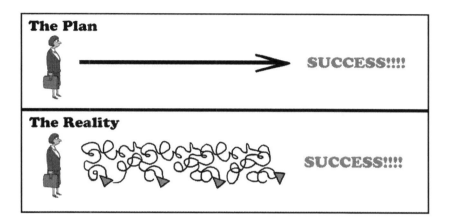

HOW TO EXPAND YOUR TARGET AUDIENCE: SLOW GROWTH

Writers always believe that they can become a bestseller if they only goose their sales properly. I actually had a brand-new writer scream at me once about this very thing. Back in the early days of Amazon's Kindle, she had "sold" 50,000 copies of her only novel by giving it away for free.

"I'll take my fifty-thousand sales over your sales any day," she shouted at me.

I said, calmly, "Talk to me in five years," and walked away.

Four years later, she's nowhere to be seen. She managed to write one more book under that name, tried the same technique with a brand-new name, wrote one or two more books, and when she realized she hadn't made more than pocket change on all of it, quit writing altogether. I have no idea what she's doing now.

Years ago, when I encountered writers like her, I'd feel bad when they quit. They were usually good writers who claimed they dreamed of writing since childhood. Yet when they realized that writing and selling books isn't as easy as reading and buying books, these writers quit.

I have learned that it's better to let these writers go and try other things. Writing was one stop on their journey, not the journey itself.

Why am I telling you this? Because so many of the gurus that have come along since the advent of the Kindle have also vanished. Or, like the marketing guru that I heard recently on a podcast, they've revamped their business to focus on production, not on marketing.

In nonbusiness terms, focusing on production means writing the next book. And the next. And the next.

However, writers do need to do some minimal marketing these days. I cover that in my book *Discoverability*, and I cover some of it earlier in this book.

I also discussed it in the previous chapter on how to expand your audience. Please go read that chapter now.

Before I started writing this chapter, I Googled the topic, just to see if I could find some current research. Instead, I found dozens of articles that offer generic business advice, and they all start with the same thing I mentioned in the previous chapter: make sure you're ready to expand your reach.

That woman who screamed at me? She wasn't ready to give her book away to anyone, let alone 50,000 potential readers. Because she didn't have a follow-up book. Even if those readers had read her novel, they couldn't buy her next, because she didn't have a next.

I tell writers to have at least ten books before they start into the free route. If the writers are writing in a series, then they need to have at least four books before giving the first away free. And never do permafree on any of your books at an ebook retailing site (like Amazon or Kobo). That limits the promotions that you can do with the book. If you want readers to get your book for free, make them come to your website and download the book there. A link to Book-Funnel will make the download easy and will also enable you to capture the email addresses of the people who downloaded, so you can send a specific newsletter to them when the next book comes out.

Make it clear on your website that downloading the book means these people are volunteering their names and email addresses for a newsletter. If you don't, the newsletter services will mark you as spam.

There. I've just given you one tip on how to expand your audience. But rather than dispense tips, I'm going to show you a game plan on how to design your own marketing for slow growth.

First, let's talk terminology. When I'm discussing marketing in this chapter and the next, I mean actual marketing. Promotion, advertising, newsletters, videos, that sort of thing. I do not mean blurbs on the back of your book or designing a cover. I assume you'll do those things as a matter of course.

Marketing, for the purposes of these next two chapters, is unusual, active behavior, behavior that other businesses would hire, say, an advertising agency to do or a marketing person in a publishing house.

Also, for the sake of these two chapters, I'm going to assume a few things. I'm going to assume that you have written and published more than one book. I'm going to assume you did the work I assigned you in the second target audience chapter and actually figured out who your current audience is. I'm going to assume that you want to keep the newcomers and that you want them to become loyal to your brand.

I'm also going to assume that you've evaluated your business and determined that you're ready to grow the audience.

As marketer Tracey Wallace wrote several years ago when she was still blogging for Mashable, "...you need to be secure in your own market before expanding to a new one. The trick to expanding is to never take too much focus off what drew customers to you in the first place. Otherwise, you risk losing them (and thereafter, your business)."[43]

153

The Mashable article—in fact, all of the articles I found about expanding an audience assume that the business needs to develop new products or move into a new neighborhood to expand the business's reach. That's true of most retail business, but not necessarily true of writers.

Books are—and have been—so poorly marketed that most existing books never reach an audience that would enjoy them. Because book marketing was always based on velocity—selling a book to a lot of people fast, and then assuming the book was "over" a few months after release—most books (including most bestsellers) never reached full market penetration.

Ah, hell, let's be honest here. Most books were never targeted at a market at all. Books received a genre label (and remember, genre is a sales tool, not a definition), a genre cover, a few marketing dollars, and a general push to the genre's readers and that was it. Traditional publishers still do that.

Indies do it, too, only they use key words and copy each other's covers and branding ideas. Indies believe that if they want to expand their reach, they need to write in a whole new genre. (Well, I've heard some writers say, urban fantasy didn't work for me. All the shifter types have been taken. So I'm going to write billionaire erotica! Sigh.)

Your game plan shouldn't be trying an entirely new type of product (unless writing in a new genre interests you). Your marketing game plan should be to slowly expand your audience with your existing books.

How do you do it?

Here's where I could do what the marketing gurus do and tell you fifteen tricks that are guaranteed to work right now.

The problem is that there's really no guarantee except this one: the tricks probably won't work six months from now. They'll be useless to you, because there will be a newer, bigger, hotter marketing trick by then.

I'll touch on hot marketing tricks in this chapter, and I'll teach you how to use those tricks as they are designed in the next chapter. But first...

The Game Plan

1. Figure out how much time you're going to invest in your marketing.

This is weekly or monthly time. Are you going to have a marketing hour every day? A marketing day every week? A marketing weekend every month? A marketing week every quarter? Figure it out, and hold to that. Don't do any marketing at any other point. You're heading for slow-growth, not rapid growth. You need to plan things that will fit into your timeline and still give you hours and hours to write and publish.

Your schedule is under your control. Pick the least disruptive option for the way that you do business.

2. Decide what you want from your marketing.

Yes, yes, I know. You want to grow your audience. But what segment of your audience do you want to grow? I mentioned in a previous chapter that my traditional publisher didn't market my African-American detective novels to African-Americans, so when I got my rights back, I focused strongly on marketing to that demographic, particularly readers.

You probably know where there are gaps in your market. Maybe you want older readers for your acclaimed YA series. Or maybe you want to widen your readership in Australia.

Once you have figured out who you're targeting, then you set up a plan. That plan will be unique to whatever group you want to expand. It's not going to be a one-size-fits-all plan.

In my case, I targeted African-American book clubs, so that

readers could discuss the series, the writer, and the choices. Cush City provided a great book club list for just that purpose. I also bought BookBubs (and BookBub lights) for the first book in the series and placed the book not in the mystery category, but in the African-American category.

I did other promotions as well, but these were the ones I started with.

You're now the Director of Marketing for your publishing company. So direct your marketing.

3. Pick one book or one series to focus on at a time.

If you're like me, you'll have a dozen different projects going at any given moment. I rotate my own marketing to fit whatever book/project is coming out this month or this year. I have a marketing game plan for that project, and I do my best to hit that plan.

I don't worry about the other projects during that time.

It's a little disingenuous to say I only focus on one. I don't. I have many projects premiering in a year, so some of my marketing plans overlap.

Sometimes, that's serendipity. When I initially wrote this chapter as a blog post, I was doing some minor marketing on my Diving series. In September, a new book, *The Runabout*, appeared. That book went up for preorder about the time I wrote that post, and I let the Diving newsletter know about it. I also posted a blog about the preorder on Tuesday.

I've posted about *The Runabout* before, because early this year it became the first full novel ever published in its entirety in *Asimov's*. That publication was great—I got reviews, some new fans, and... many many many pages of advertising in that magazine. The best kind of advertising, the kind where people actually read my work and decide if they like it.

So I've done small marketing on *The Runabout* before the book officially appeared. I did a fuller press in September. WMG sent out review copies. Audible is promoting the audiobook because it was produced by Audible Studios. So there's a lot of marketing already going on.

And...something else came up. About a year ago, I noted that writers were doing starter kit bundles for their book series. You want to get into a long series? Buy the first three books as a bundle.

I suggested to WMG that we do that with all of our series. Allyson Longueira, WMG's publisher, decided that she could allot only so much staff time to the project, so the bundles have appeared slowly—one, two, or three a month.

That, plus a "bundle" of the Uncollected Anthology that I'm a part of, and seeing some gorgeous short story bundles that friends were putting together made me think of curating a bundle of bundles for Storybundle. That went live at the same time as the original blog post for this chapter. I had a lot of choices for which one of my own starter kits to include, but I decided on Diving because...you know...*The Runabout*. So, I figured, let's get some new readers on board before the book came out.

I'm in a lot of Storybundles in 2017 because of WMG. Dean or Allyson or someone (I can't remember) came up with the idea of organizing Storybundles around *Fiction River* volumes (Dean and I are the series editors and masterminds behind *Fiction River*).

Limited time bundles, like Storybundle, enable writers to band together to promote each other's work. We end up sharing readers. The readers decide if they want to continue with the new-to-them authors' work.

The sharing doesn't happen quickly. Readers take their own sweet time to sample works by writers unfamiliar to them. About a third of bundle purchasers get to everything within the month. The rest take a year or more—or never get to the purchase.

How do I know this? Not just because readers write to me and tell me when (if) they plan to buy the bundle. (The morning I wrote the original post, someone emailed to say she had to read the previous bundles before buying a new one.)

That's anecdotal stuff. I have actual data. This spring, WMG included an online lecture through Teachable [44] [link] in one of the bundles I curated. That lecture had a specific download code, good for a long time. The bundle ended, we know how many bundles were sold, and how many of those people have used the code.

I've seen similar things with first books in a series that appeared in a bundle, but spread across multiple platforms. The bundles, like anything that involves reading or actually consuming the product, take a lot more time than free downloads do, but they produce better results.

Remember, our goal in growing our audience isn't just to get names on a list. Our goal is to make readers who will return whenever you produce another book. That's why I prefer things that encourage newcomers to read my books and stories, as opposed to things that simply get me a bunch of names.

You'll note, though, that I cited data above. I've alluded to other data as well. Data are very important when you're doing actual marketing and here's why.

4. Test, evaluate, decide.

Once you figure out what you want to do, you'll try all kinds of marketing strategies. Because your time is limited, you'll only do one or two at a time.

Consider your first foray into a certain marketing strategy a test. Figure out how you can evaluate that test, using data that our internet world so freely makes available.

Once the test is completed, decide if the marketing method is something you want to repeat, modify, or discard. Again, that's something only you can decide.

In March of 2017, Ron Vitale wrote a marvelous blog about precisely this process.[45] He had decided to use Instafreebie six months earlier after hearing great things about it, and how well it worked. He had set goals for the Instafreebie experiment, goals that the experiment hit only partially.

Then he had to evaluate whether he would be better off spending that time and money on Instafreebie or on some other marketing strategy. I'll keep you in suspense about his decision because I want you to read his blog. I want you to see how this kind of marketing experiment works, and what kind of thinking you should put into it.

5. Keep your ear to the ground.

Marketing is often about trying something different, not about following the crowd. That said, the crowd sometimes has great ideas.

In my weekly blog, I complain a lot about the "current gurus" but partly because I'm constantly listening to them. Most of these people have only written a handful of books (if that). Their success comes from extreme marketing. If I only had one or two books, I could really focus down on marketing as well. (And I'd be the most miserable person on Planet Earth. I love writing. I like marketing—sometimes. At every full moon on every fifth month. Maybe.)

Sometimes, though, those extreme marketing gambits contain the nugget of a good idea. After listening to the Amazon ad gurus, I urged WMG to try Amazon ads. We're doing ads slowly (a few per month) and leaving them up. We're finding a sweet spot, but we've only put up twenty-one of our books so far (out of 600) because life's too short.

I also put together something as I listened to the folks who kept saying the ads worked. They were nonfiction writers who had one or two novels. So, I wondered, was it their nonfiction that sold through the ads?

We put up some nonfiction books after that little realization, and voila! the sales off the ads for those books were much higher than the fiction sales. But we're using Amazon ads for something other than direct sales. We're using them as advertising, and advertising (as those of you who've read *Discoverability* know) is all about eyeballs and impressions and being out there, not about one-to-one direct sales.

Because of the internet, you can find out about the latest hottest trend the week it becomes the latest, hottest. You can try old things as well. You can find all kinds of ways to promote. BookBub's blog often lists some of the current hot things [46], and many are worth experimenting over. For example, BookBub's blog included fascinating ideas after Book Expo, some of which I want to try.[47] They do this sort of blog often, and it's worth investigating.

6. Keep an eye on the culture.

Every fall, a new TV show takes over the culture. That show might dovetail with a book you wrote. I tried to get my old traditional publisher to market my fairy tale books to the *Once Upon A Time* crowd when that series started, but noooo. Specificity would have been too hard for my traditional publisher.

By the time I got the rights, *Once Upon A Time* wasn't as hot, and there were other things to focus on.

Zombies were hot for a while. If you had a zombie book, then promoting it to *The Walking Dead* fans was a good idea. Or runners who used the Zombies, Run! app. (And if you want to learn more about marketing and business read this Lifehacker piece about the app.[48]) Advertising your book on an app or partnering with the app (in the case of Zombies, Run!) by offering the book as a contest reward, would be a great marketing strategy.

TV, movies, games, apps—popular culture is always obsessing about something, and if your work ties into that something, then promote it in the moment.

Be creative. Be fearless. Have fun.

7. Be the first writer to try this.

I read *Adweek* a lot, always scouring the ways that other businesses in the entertainment industry are doing their marketing. *Adweek* has many free newsletters, and I swear I get an idea a week from at least one of them. Some of those ideas cost too much money to execute (right now) and some would cost too much time. But some spark low-cost ideas for me or have a nugget based in the middle that I hadn't considered before.

I also learn things that are broader than how to market my books, like the importance of branding throughout a company. As I mentioned earlier in this book, Syfy changed its branding and its programming—and I discovered this through *Adweek*.

A lot of writers have made a name for themselves as marketers because they were the first—the first to do bookmarks (Debbie Macomber), the first to do TV ads (James Patterson). You know you've hit something when you get a good result. Then it's up to you whether or not to share it.

8. Realize that good results might not be replicable.

Sometimes surprise is the most important thing. Or, sometimes promotions work for one book and won't work for another. You can do great things with the first book in a series that you can't do with later books. That's why I tell you not to make that first book permafree. There are a million marketing opportunities—advertising opportunities—that go by the wayside when you have that book forever free. Bundles are one. A BOGO sale is another. There are many, many more.

Some promotions work well in one genre and don't work at all for another one. And some worked great in 2012 and don't work at all now, like Kindle's free bestseller list. Five years ago, readers read the free books and then moved to the author's other works. Not so much any more.

Some promotions really are a function of the time and place. (See #6 above)

9. Realize you can't do everything.

After you start exercising your promotion muscle, you'll start getting more ideas than you can possibly execute. Do the ones that fit into your schedule and your budget. Then use the data to figure out if you're investing your time wisely.

10. Some (most) promotions will fail.

Especially if you haven't defined your goal for that promotion. If your goal is to grow your audience, then keep that as your focus always. If the promotion doesn't actually grow your readership, which you can measure by increased book sales, then dump the promotion, no matter how many names it adds to your newsletter or how many free downloads people have taken.

11. Measure your overall success in months and years, not in days and weeks.

Your goal is to increase your readership over time. So, if you do successful promotions, your sales should be greater (on those projects) than they were at the same time the year before (barring unforeseens in the culture like nasty elections or major terror attacks, things that make people watch the tube instead of read). Greater than might be a hundred sales greater than or several thousand greater than.

Your growth pattern will not be a straight line. It'll be a series of waves, with plateaus and downturns. But you should, overall, end up with more readers than you started with.

Slow growth means exactly that. You're growing your business—your customer base, your loyal reader base—a little bit at a time.

The business world has another term for slow growth. You'll often hear the word "sustainable" in connection with expanding a business. Rapid growth isn't sustainable, and can often hurt an unprepared business. Even slow growth can be hard to maintain at times.

But slow growth is sustainable. It's not predictable, but it is something that you can maintain over months and even years.

The coolest thing about slow growth is that moment when you realize that you have way more readers than you ever thought you did. You weren't tracking them day to day or obsessing about them. You just noticed on the way to doing something else.

Keep your focus on growing your audience, manage your time wisely, and write the next book. If you do those things over the space of years, you'll still be writing and publishing five years from now. If you don't control your time and you forget to write, you'll be doing something else—like that woman who screamed at me.

She failed. Not as a promoter, but as a writer. And she didn't fail because she made mistakes marketing.

She failed because she quit writing. She quit trying.

That's the only way to fail in this business.

So experiment with marketing. Have fun with it.

Just like you have fun with your writing.

"Our marketing expansion seems a little haphazard."

HOW TO EXPAND YOUR TARGET AUDIENCE: AGGRESSIVE GROWTH

Here's the surprising chapter. Many people who read my blog regularly probably think that I'm opposed to major marketing campaigns. I'm not. I'm opposed to them when they're done incorrectly.

What's incorrectly?

Pretty much everything you see from traditional publishing to most indies. You have to look outside of publishing to see how to do a smart, aggressive growth campaign designed to grow an audience.

Why do I say traditional publishing and most writers do it wrong? Because...(wait for it)...an aggressive campaign to grow your target audience is part of a long-term strategy.

Publishing has turned aggressive growth campaigns into a short-term strategy, one that has no real upside.

Here's what I mean.

Traditional publishing in modern times is based on the velocity model—selling a lot of books fast, then ignoring the product, and moving to another product.

Standard business growth is the exact opposite. You develop

your company, develop your brand, cultivate your consumers, and then, once your business is large enough, consider making that business bigger.

When you decide the time is right to aggressively grow your audience, you should pull out every trick in the book and design a few of your own. You will work very hard on getting people to sample your wares. Most of the people who try your books will not continue reading them. Most people—because they didn't like the book they sampled or they have only so much time or other favorite authors—will not return to your other work right away. And that's okay, because your efforts here should have netted you 5 to 10 percent of the readers you targeted.

In other words, a properly done aggressive growth campaign will get you more readers. If you're inexperienced with growing your readership, you'll be disappointed. Not by the results on this book, but on the next one.

Writers never think of comparing the sales of the book before the growth-campaign to the sales of the book published after the campaign ends. But those are the important numbers.

Let me make up some numbers to show you what I mean.

Let's say you've published a series of books. Each book in the series stands alone, like books in mystery or romance series do. You decide to do an aggressive growth campaign for book six. You've had steady readership growth with books one through five.

Book five's sales were about 10,000 copies (over the first three months after release). Please note that I picked 10,000 copies because the math is easy, not because I know something about average series sales.

You do your variation of an aggressive growth campaign. Your goal is to get book six in front of hundreds of thousand of potential readers. You hope that 100,000 will actually buy the book, over and above your 10,000 loyal readers—and you're successful.

In the first three months of release, you sell 110,000 copies of book six.

Fast forward to book seven, which comes out a year later. (Why a year? Because you spent so damn much time marketing. Ideal strategy would be six months later, but we'll ignore that for the moment.)

In the first three months of its release, book seven sells 20,000 copies. Double what book five sold before your massive marketing push. Yet most writers would be horribly disappointed. Most traditional publishers would cancel the series right then and there, declaring it a failure.

But you're an indie writer, not someone in traditional publishing. Books one through five are still in print.

Readers are not predictable folk. So, of the 100,000 new readers who bought the book, 50,000 actually read it in a timely fashion (meaning the first three months). Twenty-five-thousand read it eventually, and 25,000 more might get to it one day.

Already your "readership" is down to 75,000, and one-third of them might not have read the book they own by the time the new book comes out. Generally speaking, the release of a new book reminds slow readers that they already own one of your books, and they should read it now.

Of the 50,000 who've read book six by the time book seven comes out, 10,000 were unimpressed and will not buy your next. Another 10,000 liked it, but not enough to run right out and get another book with your byline. The remaining 30,000 split in a variety of directions.

Some read the series from the beginning. Some go back to book five. Some buy book seven and forget all about books one through five.

You can measure some of this. After a huge marketing push on book six, you will see a lump of readers work their way through the entire series. Even if the series is compelling, the lump will spread out over time. Why? Because some readers don't like binging. So they'll read one of your books, then five books by other writers, then another of your books, then ten books by other writers—and so on.

You can't predict how all readers will read. What you can do is make sure you have a lot of books available, so that the readers who discovered you in the big marketing push have a lot of product to choose from after they've finished the initial book.

And that's where traditional publishing falls down. They don't brand anything in a series, and stupidly, they take books out of print or make the books hard to find or keep the high ebook prices on backlist, so readers will find less expensive reads elsewhere.

If some of a traditionally published writer's books are with a different traditional publisher, the publisher who does the huge push tries hard not to mention the writer's other works. Which is stupid, but it's modern business.

It hurts not only the new publisher, but the writer as well.

So...indies...you want to run an aggressive marketing campaign. You want to spend a lot of time promoting your latest novel, and you want to grow your readership fast.

Here's what you need first:

You need a lot of product

An aggressive growth campaign is not something a new writer should do. By a lot, I'd say you need at least five books in your ongoing series.

Or, if you're doing trilogies, you need two completed trilogies before designing an aggressive growth campaign for the first book in your newest trilogy.

If you're writing standalone books, then you need at least ten (hopefully in the same genre), so that readers have a lot of choice to buy more books of yours once they've finished the book you've put all your marketing dollars behind.

You need a realistic goal

Are you running an aggressive growth campaign because "everyone does it" or because someone told you that you needed to get a lot of readers fast or because you're emulating traditional publishing? If so, abandon this idea now.

Your goal needs to be concrete for your business. I can think of two great reasons to run an aggressive growth campaign.

Reason One: You want readers to learn that you (or your series or your book) exist. This is an informational campaign, targeting at making potential readers notice you when they haven't noticed you in the past. You'll get new readers here, but generally speaking, you won't get a one-to-one growth. By that I mean, you will not get one reader for each dollar spent. You may not see how the money you've spent translates into readers for months. This is how traditional publishing used to market books in the 1960s, when traditional publishing did marketing better than they do now. This is how books like *Catch-22*, which only sold 7,500 copies in that all important first month, became long-term bestsellers.

Because the publishers back then invested in aggressive marketing techniques on the books they believed in for months after publication—if not years.

Your goal, when you do an informational campaign, is long-term. You want people to notice you, keep noticing you, and finally cave in and buy the book they've "been hearing so much about."

Reason Two: You want to actively put the book in the hands of readers, get reviews, get word-of-mouth going, and essentially give the book away. This can be a double-edged sword, because the readers and the reviewers and anyone who gets the book might end up hating it.

However, you do not give the book away for free...except to targeted power readers (like the owners of bookstores [yes, there still are bookstores]). You reduce the price of the book and do major promotional campaigns like BookBubs and other short-term strategies that I'll mention briefly below.

The goal of this strategy is to get a reader to sample one novel of yours from beginning to end. You have to trust your skills enough to believe that once the reader finishes the book, they will want another one of your books. And when they finish that book, they will want another and another.

The readership numbers I mentioned at the beginning of this post? That's what usually happens with this kind of aggressive growth campaign.

Back to the things you need before you start executing the campaign.

You need a budget

Yes, budget first before your game plan. And the budget has to be a two-fold budget.

Budget 1: You need a financial budget for your campaign. Are you going to spend $5,000 growing your audience? $10,000? $20,000? $100,000?

You need to realistically set this budget, and you need to stick to it.

You will not be able to do everything you want to do—no one has an unlimited advertising budget, not even movie studios. You work within the budget you have, and make the best choices you can based on that budget.

Budget 2: You need a time budget for your campaign. If you're running the campaign—and most indies will be doing this alone—then you need to set aside a certain number of hours per day or per week to work on this campaign. You will be spending a lot of time on marketing, and to do this right, you will probably be losing writing time.

Losing writing time will cost you money in the long term. You have to factor that financial loss into your business's annual budget. (Not in the advertising budget.) You will not make up this financial loss even if you gain new readers—not that fast, anyway. Over time you might.

But better to be prepared than to be upset at the lost writing time.

You need a timeline

This aggressive growth campaign will last for a finite period of time. You can pick anything from one to six months. But do not go past six months. People will get heartily sick of you flogging this book if you're doing it longer than six months.

In fact, I initially wanted to tell you to do no more than three months, but that's not realistic. Some of the strategies for this kind of campaign take months of prep time. You want to place a banner ad on NPR? They only have so much space and a lot of competition for that space. Plus they have rules about the specs for the ad and you might not hit that the first time. (Note that I am not talking about the Google ads you see on the websites you go to if you don't have your ad blocker on, but the ads you see even with the ad blocker, the ones built into the site itself.)

There is a sweet spot between getting people's attention and annoying the heck out of them. It depends on the product and what you're going to do with the ad.

Here's how I would develop a timeline on a major aggressive growth campaign:

Pre-Timeline: Research all the methods of promotion you're interested in. Try a few in your slow-growth plan to see if those methods are all hype or if they actually work. If you are partnering with others—running ads or publishing bundled stories—figure out their deadlines and specifications.

Month One: Mail Advance Reading Copies, get your preorder(s) up if you plan to do that, prepare your ads, get your partners lined up (whoever they might be).

Month Two: Get readers to begin word of mouth, do some prepublication work (if you're doing this before publication), maybe give some related fiction away free on your website, use older works to beef up your newsletter—maybe even start a new newsletter and do a special promotion to get those thousands of names that some people taunt. Learn Google, Facebook, and Amazon ads if you haven't already done that, make sure your website is spiffy, your Facebook Page ready, and so on.

Month Three: Launch the book and the campaign, do all the special things you've planned, maybe cycle through BookBub and BookBub light, buy TV ads, radio ads, or whatever big expenditures you're going to do.

Month Four: The second half of your campaign here, whatever that might be. Make sure you've included something unique to you and your project, something memorable that no one else has done.

Month Five: Slow back down to your normal slow-growth advertising, gather your analytics.

Month Six: Review the campaign, write it up internally so that you have notes on how it went for future campaigns. List what worked and what didn't. Plan to revisit the analytics three months from now to see if there are surprises.

Note in my timeline there's only two intense months of visible promotion. In this case, I scheduled them around the publication of the book. But you can do this same kind of promotion around an existing book. You don't have to do it on release. For example, if you published a Christmas book in 2015 in a series that you're still continuing, you might want to center a major aggressive growth campaign around that Christmas book, and make sure the visible part of your marketing happens in November and early December.

Your only limit here is your imagination (and your time and your budget).

You need to be traditional

Figure out what kind of book marketing works for you as a reader, then replicate it. Try the things you've heard about. Do what you always wanted a traditional publisher to do, but you couldn't get them to do it. Do review copies for established review publications that handle your genre. If you're writing literary fiction, send ARCs to the *New York Times* or work with the American Booksellers Association's Red Box program to get the attention of bookstores. If you're writing genre fiction, then get your review copies to the leading bloggers and review magazines, even if you think there's no hope of a review.

You're going for attention here, and you're spending some money. Do the thing readers expect. Some regular readers will find you. I find books bimonthly from *Mystery Scene Magazine*—their print edition. I know others do, too. Figure that out for yourself.

You need to be creative

I've been saying throughout this book that traditional publishers have no idea how to market any more. I've said that for years, but the impetus of this series came from the Targoz Reading Pulse survey. What inspired me the most in that survey was a category called "Media Reach by Genre."[49] The Survey, remember, interviewed readers and nonreaders alike and found out what their interests were—outside of book publishing.

Why is this important? Because it helps you be creative.

For example, the survey found that romance readers watch more television than the average person, but their viewing habits are pretty specific. They do watch network television, but they don't watch Fox. They don't watch much cable TV—except for Lifetime. Almost half of romance readers watch Lifetime once a week.

Other notable things in this section about romance readers include the fact that they read the print version of *People* magazine. One in three romance readers read *People* every week—and actually read it. They don't just buy it.

And then there's this lovely statistic: 64 percent of romance readers read their local print newspaper every week and 47 percent read the online version.

In fact, this section notes that almost all readers read their local newspaper, either online or in print. (Depends on the readers' preferred genre as to where or how much they read in their local paper.)

I read those statistics and did a literal head slap. I've worked in local media off and on my whole life. WMG's publisher, Allyson Longueira, used to run the local newspaper. Local papers—particularly those in smaller communities—are always searching for good hooks for articles. What better than a local author who has a new book release—particularly if that local author is going to buy a print ad to go along with that story?

Cable stations like Lifetime have slots for local advertising. They also have places on their websites for local promotions. Target your audience, and develop an ad.

Or, if you're writing a cozy mystery filled with recipes, hold a party at a local hotel in which local chefs do a cook-off from your recipes. Give away copies of your book, and invite all of the local media to attend from the TV stations to the radio stations. Get friends to live-tweet the event, and run the event live in Google Events or on Facebook.

As I said above, you're limited only by your imagination. (And your time and your budget.)

You need to be unique

Go outside the norm and do something really unusual. The chef idea above is one of those, but there are a million ways to do this.

In the book, *Avid Reader*, publisher Robert Gottlieb—who was one of those megamarketers who invented most of modern book marketing—talked about the marketing campaign for *Catch-22*. In the early 1960s, they put postage-paid comment cards inside the hardcover copy of the books, asking readers to fill out the card with their opinions of the book and send the cards back. Gottlieb then did an entire six-month marketing campaign filled with reader comments.

That's so much easier today. Develop a hashtag for your book and at the end of the book, ask for reader comments along with that hashtag. Or do a group reading of the book (everyone read at the same time) and then live tweet as they go along (this is not for the faint of heart; you will see stuff you don't want to see).

Memorable campaigns will stick in the reader's mind. I went back to the Gottlieb book because he mentioned that one of the big supporters of *Catch-22* was NBC News anchor John Chancellor. On his own dime, Chancellor created thousands of "Yossarian Lives" stickers, which college students then used to deface buildings and tables and books. I remember going to universities years later and finding "Yossarian Lives" stickers on library carrels or inside bathroom stalls. That campaign went on forever—and created a life of its own.

On the day I wrote this chapter, I logged onto Twitter for my usual 140-character dose of culture (or not), and discovered a unique marketing campaign for *Guardians of The Galaxy Vol. 2*. Just in time for the streaming release (August 8, 2017) and the Blu-ray version (later this month), the team that brought you the movie did a three-minute cheesy music video.

The video is in keeping with the offbeat tone of the movies. Since the music in both movies is deliberately 1970s (for a plot reason), this video harks back to those 1970s dance shows that most of you are too young to remember.

This is pure marketing, designed to go viral, and to give the fans something fun and interesting. Now I will help the video go viral by sharing it in the endnotes.[50]

Why did I share it? Because this is what I mean by unique. Sure, sure, other movie promotions will do something similar as soon as this fall because this worked. But they won't be as fun or interesting, and probably won't be as memorable either.

This is what I mean by "be unique."

And have fun.

You need to brand your marketing campaign

And this is where the happy music comes to a screeching halt.

Wha…Wha…What? You ask.

Haven't you ever noticed that all major marketing campaigns have a theme? A look? A brand?

If you're doing this to increase the readership of your series, then you can brand the campaign to reflect the series. But you can only do that once. You'll need to come up with a whole new brand the next time you do a major marketing campaign.

All of the stuff we talked about with branding itself, way back at the beginning of this book—all of that applies to an aggressive growth campaign. *All* of it. From the look to the target audience to the taglines to marketing to the right places, your campaign has to be a thing just like your book is a thing.

And they should really be separate—in that, a good campaign

should reflect your book or your style, but be a creative endeavor all its own.

You need to end your campaign

It has to have a limited shelf life, never to be repeated. Not just because of your timeline, but because the moment marketing becomes repetitive, people tune it out.

Besides, you need to end your campaign because you have a life and you have books to write.

You need to use data to determine your campaign's success

Everything you did might meet the goals you set for the campaign. Or, just as likely, everything you did might fail.

That's called a learning curve, folks.

And the reason I mention the learning curve is because...

You need to learn from this effort

You might learn that aggressive growth campaigns aren't for you. You might learn that you love aggressive growth campaigns more than you like writing. You might learn that aggressive growth campaigns work for you.

You might learn that you had a semi-successful campaign and you want to change a few things should you do it all over again.

If you are successful, realize not all of that success will be replicable. Some of it will work because you're the first to do it (Guardians Inferno) and some of it will work because you're using tried-and-true methods and some of it will work because people were bored in August of 2017 and your campaign was able to cut through the noise.

Make notes about the things that you think will work in the future, and chalk the rest of it up to learning.

You need to take a long break

If you're going to incorporate aggressive growth campaigns into building your target audience and ultimately your brand, realize that this is a tool you should unleash rarely.

If you do a big aggressive growth campaign every time you release a book, people will expect it of you and at some point, you won't be able to deliver.

Better to do an aggressive growth campaign every few years, once it has become clear that your previous campaign has plateaued. The data will not accurately reflect a plateau for at least a year, maybe more. So continue with your slow-growth campaign, write a lot of books, and come back to this when there are new tricks and techniques that other people have pioneered that you want to try.

Or when you have time to burn, or $10,000 to burn.

Or, maybe you'll want to hire a staff to do a campaign for you. I tried this several years ago, and it was an unmitigated disaster. That was primarily my fault because I hired the wrong people to do the work (a distinct possibility whenever you hire someone). I've done smaller things since with a much newer, much better team, and that seems to be working out.

One secret

You can do a half-assed aggressive growth campaign. You target a few things that you've always wanted to do, and throw some time and money at them.

WMG Publishing did a small aggressive growth campaign this fall for my latest Nelscott novel, *Protectors*. The book is the beginning of a new series, but it's related to the Smokey Dalton series, so fans should find it interesting.

But we needed to inform a slightly different audience about the book, so our entire campaign is about getting out the word that the book exists. Oh, and that it's unlike anything anyone has done before. And that it is related to the previous Kris Nelscott books in setting and with one familiar character.

I'll report on the marketing of all of this about a year from now, once we see what's happened. The book just went up for pre-order (as I initially wrote this chapter). I got a proof of the paper Advance Reading Copy today (the ebook ARC went out weeks ago), and we're having a meeting next week to tweak our strategy.

This is not a major tens of thousands of dollars campaign because we don't have the time, but it is a six-month awareness campaign that will take more time and more dollars than any campaign we did before.

It's not quite what I'm talking about in this blog, but it's close.

Aggressive growth campaigns are not for the faint of heart or the weak of wallet. These campaigns take time, money, and a lot of creativity to pull off well.

If you're going to do one, make sure you have a lot of marketing under your belt. Also make sure you know what you want from the campaign. Be prepared to throw thousands of dollars into the mix without seeing any results at all.

Also be prepared to have a lot of success. Because that can happen with aggressive growth campaigns. Make sure you can handle the growth.

With writers, that's relatively easy—if you've done what I listed first. You need a lot of product, so that the readers who joined up in this campaign have other reading material of yours while they wait for the next book of yours.

Remember all those lists in brick-and-mortar stores in the early days of Harry Potter? If you liked Harry Potter, you'll like this fantasy series by this other author? Those existed because by book three, it became clear that these voracious Harry Potter readers needed something to tide them over to the next Harry Potter book a year away.

You want people to use your backlist to tide them over until the next book in your series. You can do that now, thanks to the fact that books can remain in print permanently these days.

Use that to your advantage.

So, essentially, if you want to do some major aggressive growth campaign, your timeline should start years ahead of the campaign. Make sure you've written the books. Then do the campaign.

Write many more books and do another campaign.

Rinse. Repeat.

And most importantly, save your firepower until you're ready. If you're going to spend money and time on a campaign like this, do it right. Don't do it the way traditional publishers do it in 2017. Do it the way they did it in 1963.

Because, oh, did I tell you? By the six-month anniversary of the publication of *Catch-22*, when the publisher took out several full-page ads in major newspapers all over the country to promote the book's word of mouth success, the book itself had only sold 35,000 copies.

It would eventually sell millions and millions. It's never gone out of print. But in 1963, the publisher was patient, using their creativity and their campaign to slowly build the book.

That's what you'll do with any kind of growth campaign—even an aggressive one. You're building your brand slowly. One reader at a time—even when you go after a big bunch of them at once.

You have to keep them.

And remember, keeping your readers isn't about tweeting all the time or haranguing them to buy.

It's about writing good books, telling great stories, and making the readers fall in love with your work.

It's about the writing.

It always has been, and it always will be.

Enjoy.

"I know transformation isn't easy.
I pulled a muscle once."

READY, SET, GO!

And now you know everything there is to know about branding for writers, right?

Um, no. We have just scratched the surface here. What I wrote in these chapters in 2017 works in 2018 and will work in 2019. But there are a lot of techniques, new apps, and incredible opportunities that exist now for writers that didn't exist when I wrote the initial blog posts. That's why I didn't get greatly specific on techniques.

Branding is the most important marketing thing you can do for your work. It also takes a lot of time to get the right brand.

Be willing to experiment. Be willing to change. Be willing to try new things.

But most of all, have fun. Branding—and marketing—are, in their own way, as creative as writing. They're just different. And something you can noodle at as you do other things.

Keep your eyes open and look at how others do it. As I write this, I'm sitting in a café. The napkins are branded with the logo. The woman behind the counter wears a branded T-shirt that is different from the branded T-shirt another employee wears. Every sign has the logo. The wall has an artistic rendering of the name of the place. The totally delicious brownie I'm savoring (and eating here) came in a plastic wrap that has the café's logo. The only thing not branded is the cup for my iced tea. If I was in Starbucks, that cup would be branded but the brownie package wouldn't.

Each place is different. Each business is different. Each writer is different.

Learn how to be your own best marketer, something original just for what you need to do and for your work.

Surface from your writing every now and then, look around at the marketing that's everywhere in our culture, and then see what you can steal. Or what's changed since you went deep into your book.

Once you figure that out, see what you can actually do.

And after you do it...

Write more. Because that's the basis for everything.

Thanks for picking up the book! I hope it helped you switch your mindset on branding.

And good luck with your writing and marketing projects!

ENDNOTES

CHAPTER 1 - IN THE BEGINNING

[1.] www.deanwesleysmith.com/workshops/

[2.] mailchi.mp/kristinekathrynrusch/boss-returns

[3.] mailchi.mp/kristinekathrynrusch/cool-writing-news-boss-returns-and-a-bit-of-gratitude

[4.] www.readingpulse.com/

[5.] www.targoz.com/market-matters-blog/2017/4/21/voice-of-the-reader-survey-finds-rising-book-prices-are-driving-buyers-to-delay-purchases-buy-used-books-or-use-subscription-services

CHAPTER 2 - TYPES OF BRANDS

[6.] www.brickmarketing.com/define-branding.htm

[7.] www.investopedia.com/terms/b/brand.asp

[8.] www.investopedia.com/terms/b/brand-identity.asp

[9.] www.readingpulse.com

[10.] hotsheetpub.com

[11.] xoxoafterdark.com/2014/02/20/2014-belles-wheels-bus-tour

[12.] www.dummies.com/business/marketing/branding/the-types-of-brands

[13.] www.mysteryscenemag.com/store/product.php?productid=17688

CHAPTER 3 - HOW TO BUILD A BRAND: THE EARLY STAGES

[14.] businesscollective.com/7-keys-to-building-a-successful-brand

CHAPTER 4 - DEFINE YOUR TARGET AUDIENCE: THE EARLY STAGES

[15.] www.indiewire.com/2017/02/get-out-jordan-peele-interview-1201785271

[16.] www.adweek.com/digital/nfl-scores-touchdown-female-fans-159674

[17.] www.entrepreneurs-journey.com/

[18.] www.quicksprout.com/the-complete-guide-to-building-your-personal-brand-chapter-2

[19.] www.indiewire.com/2017/02/get-out-jordan-peele-interview-1201785271

CHAPTER 5: BRAND IDENTITY

[20.] www.investopedia.com/terms/b/brand-identity.asp

[21.] www.adweek.com/tv-video/in-brand-reboot-syfy-doubles-its-scripted-series-and-broadens-scope-to-include-superhero-programming

CHAPTER 6 - BRAND IMAGE

[22.] Gottlieb, Robert, *Avid Reader: A Life*, Farrar, Strauss, and Giroux, 2016, hardcover edition, p. 147

[23.] www.businessdictionary.com/definition/brand-image.html

CHAPTER 7 - BRAND LOYALTY

[24.] www.factory360.com/brand-loyalty-5-interesting-statistics

[25.] www.readingpulse.com

[26.] www.rwa.org/p/cm/ld/fid=582

[27.] www.forbes.com/sites/davidvinjamuri/2014/03/04/the-strongest-brand-in-publishing-is/#378ba5d5ebfa

28. www.behavioraleconomics.com/mini-encyclopedia-of-be/choice-overload

29. www.retentionscience.com/customer-loyalty-vs-brand-loyalty

30. www.cnbc.com/2017/05/01/why-people-keep-buying-apple-products.html

31. www.thecreativepenn.com/2017/06/12/publishing-industry-launching-non-fiction-dan-blank

32. www.forbes.com/sites/davidvinjamuri/2014/03/04/the-strongest-brand-in-publishing-is/#289bcd1eebfa

33. www.forbes.com/sites/davidvinjamuri/2014/03/04/the-strongest-brand-in-publishing-is/2/#6edc62624be6

34. www.ama.org/events-training/Conferences/Pages/secret-loyal-customers.aspx

35. www.ama.org/events-training/Conferences/Pages/secret-loyal-customers.aspx

36. www.forbes.com/sites/davidvinjamuri/2014/03/04/the-strongest-brand-in-publishing-is/2/#46e425884be6

37. factory360.com/brand-loyalty-5-interesting-statistics

CHAPTER 8 - DEFINE YOUR TARGET AUDIENCE: THE INTERMEDIATE STAGES

38. www.forbes.com/sites/bridgetbrennan/2013/03/06/the-real-reason-women-shop-more-than-men/#2d3a43e674b9

39. www.readingpulse.com

CHAPTER 9 - HOW TO BUILD A BRAND: THE INTERMEDIATE STAGES

40. www.wmgpublishinginc.com/2017/07/10/publishers-note-using-tools-for-series-branding

41. www.inc.com/geoffrey-james/how-to-build-a-strong-brand.html

42. www.audiencebloom.com/how-to-build-a-brand-from-scratch

CHAPTER 11 - HOW TO EXPAND YOUR TARGET AUDIENCE: SLOW GROWTH

43. mashable.com/2013/12/27/opening-new-market/#_6OwceMkIaqg
44. wmg-publishing-workshops-and-lectures.teachable.com
45. www.ronvitale.com/blog/2017/3/29/is-instafreebie-still-an-effective-marketing-technique
46. insights.bookbub.com/category/book-marketing-ideas
47. insights.bookbub.com/top-book-marketing-takeaways-book-expo-2017
48. lifehacker.com/behind-the-app-the-story-of-zombies-run-1632445358

CHAPTER 12 - HOW TO EXPAND YOUR TARGET AUDIENCE: AGGRESSIVE GROWTH

49. www.readingpulse.com
50. youtu.be/3MMMe1drnZY

I value honest feedback, and would love to hear your opinion in a review, if you're so inclined, on your favorite book retailer's site.

Be the first to know!

Please sign up for the Kristine Kathryn Rusch newsletter, and receive exclusive content, keep up with the latest news, releases and so much more—even the occasional giveaway.

So, what are you waiting for? To sign up go to kristinekathrynrusch.com.

But wait! There's more. Sign up for the WMG Publishing newsletter, too, and get the latest news and releases from all of the WMG authors and lines, including Kristine Grayson, Kris Nelscott, Dean Wesley Smith, *Fiction River: An Original Anthology Magazine, Smith's Monthly,* and so much more.

To sign up go to wmgpublishing.com.

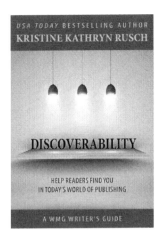

For writers, discoverability means the difference between gaining an audience and publishing into the void. *New York Times* bestselling author Kristine Kathryn Rusch deftly tackles the topic in this latest WMG Writers' Guide.

"Kristine [Kathryn Rusch]'s extensive experience in both traditional and indie publishing shines through in this amazing book. Though written for fiction authors, all writers will benefit from reading this book."

— TIM GRAHL, "11 BEST BOOK MARKETING BOOKS"

"Kristine Kathryn Rusch's new book *Discoverability* is by far the best resource I have read to date to help indie authors succeed after the book is written."

— CHRIS SYME, PRINCIPAL OF CKSYME MEDIA GROUP

ABOUT THE AUTHOR

New York Times bestselling author Kristine Kathryn Rusch writes in almost every genre. Generally, she uses her real name (Rusch) for most of her writing. Under that name, she publishes bestselling science fiction and fantasy, award-winning mysteries, acclaimed mainstream fiction, controversial nonfiction, and the occasional romance. Her novels have made bestseller lists around the world and her short fiction has appeared in eighteen best of the year collections. She has won more than twenty-five awards for her fiction, including the Hugo, *Le Prix Imaginales*, the *Asimov's* Readers Choice award, and the *Ellery Queen Mystery Magazine* Readers Choice Award.

Publications from *The Chicago Tribune* to *Booklist* have included her Kris Nelscott mystery novels in their top-ten-best mystery novels of the year. The Nelscott books have received nominations for almost every award in the mystery field, including the best novel Edgar Award, and the Shamus Award.

She writes goofy romance novels as award-winner Kristine Grayson.

She also edits. Beginning with work at the innovative publishing company, Pulphouse, followed by her award-winning tenure at *The Magazine of Fantasy & Science Fiction*, she took fifteen years off before returning to editing with the original anthology series *Fiction River,* published by WMG Publishing. She acts as series editor with her husband, writer Dean Wesley Smith, and edits at least two anthologies in the series per year on her own.

To keep up with everything she does, go to kriswrites.com and sign up for her newsletter. To track her many pen names and series, see their individual websites (krisnelscott.com, kristinegrayson.com, krisdelake.com, retrievalartist.com, divingintothewreck.com).

Keep informed:
www.kriswrites.com